GOOD BOSSES DO

GOOD BOSSES DO

HOW TO FIND, HIRE, AND KEEP A GOOD SECRETARY

BETSY LAZARY CPS

amacom

American Management Association

11-29-01

This book is available at a special discount
when ordered in bulk quantities.
For information, contact Special Sales Department,
AMACOM, a division of American Management Association,
135 West 50th Street, New York, NY 10020.

Library of Congress Cataloging-in-Publication Data

Lazary, Betsy.
   Good bosses do.

   Includes index.
   1. Secretaries—Recruiting. 2. Secretaries.
I. Title.
HF5547.5.L36 1988   658.4'09   87-47850
ISBN 0-8144-5917-X

Printing number

10 9 8 7 6 5 4 3 2 1

To my husband, Carl, without whom this book could never have been written. . .and to my son, Andrew, in spite of whom this book was somehow written.

Preface

During my career as a secretary, I was lucky to have worked with more bosses who valued secretaries than with those who did not. Looking back, however, it's clear that all of my accomplishments were qualified by, "not bad for a secretary." Even though I was proud of my contributions, I unconsciously caught on to the general opinion of those around me that if I thought anything of myself, I'd get out of secretarial work. So I worked hard, got a degree, and broke out of the secretarial mold. Then I decided to help other secretaries do the same thing, and StepTakers, my company, was born.

As I studied the issues that keep secretaries from getting ahead, I became more aware of what comprises the secretary's role in an organization and came to realize just how essential the secretary's function is to a manager's success. As my understanding grew, StepTakers evolved, no longer focusing on helping secretaries out of the profession but showing them how to make the most of it.

The more I learned, the more I was convinced that secretaries *do* make a significant, valuable contribution, only few people—including many secretaries themselves—seemed to realize that fact. Or if they did, it certainly wasn't reflected in the way secretaries were treated. It also was readily apparent that much of the problem was directly related to the simple fact that most managers just don't know how to work with a secretary. It's an area of training that has until now been completely overlooked.

And something was in the wind. Secretaries were no longer the only ones complaining; managers were also lamenting that it was becoming increasingly difficult to find a good secretary. More frequently, managers themselves, not just secretaries, were turning to StepTakers for solutions to secretarial problems. It seemed the time was ripe for addressing issues that affect secretaries and managers alike. Managers finally seemed ready to listen.

I don't belong to that group of doomsayers who believe that managers won't change. I think managers have no choice but to respond to what the environment requires—if they want to succeed in today's competitive business world. I believe there are solutions to the secretaries' plight that will benefit management and secretaries alike. And so this book was written.

Acknowledgments

In expressing appreciation, it's necessary to start at the beginning. Going way back, thanks to Alvin M. Stein, a great boss who knows the value of a secretary, for starting me off on the right foot. Thanks to Joan Etzel for the initial push and sense of direction in starting this project, and to brother Michael Lazary for enthusiasm and encouragement in the outline stages.

Many thanks to friends and colleagues at Professional Secretaries International, especially the New York City Chapter, for contributed material, continued support, and shared personal experiences. Also to Tara Roth Madden and E. James Brennan, who contributed their time and expertise.

Thanks to editor Ron Mallis and agent Denise Marcil for providing the guidance and reassurance a first-time writer needs. And to Charles Singer for invaluable late-night troubleshooting, disaster saving, and when all else failed, comfort in painful lessons learned in using a computer.

Considering the project was undertaken during the first year of my first child's life, many thanks must go to family and friends who helped in the delicate balancing act. Frances Ern, Jeanette Lazary, Michael and Clarice Lazary, Angela Lazary, and Wendy Ritacco deserve special recognition for their help with Andrew. Thanks to Carl Margolin, who kept my head on straight. And to Carl Ern, husband and supporter first class, who can now write a book on what it means to be an involved father.

Contents

GOOD BOSSES DO

CHAPTER ONE

WHERE HAVE ALL THE SECRETARIES GONE?

Have you noticed it's hard to find a good secretary these days? It seems almost everyone has a disaster story to share about secretaries who haven't worked out and even worse ones who took their place. Overall, it seems nearly impossible to find that rare, highly qualified professional.

You've also probably noticed an undercurrent of dissatisfaction among secretaries. They want more money and recognition. They want to be taken seriously and appreciated. You may sympathize, yet feel it's not your problem. But the plight of the secretary *is* your problem.

Years ago, you could get by with a secretary who was pleasant enough on the phone and who could type at a decent speed. But those days are gone. Thanks to the information age, your work pace has accelerated incredibly. You need a key person to help keep you on top of your job despite those who are doing their best to beat you out. You need someone ambitious enough to keep up with you and smart enough to master your new PC.

As a top-notch secretary becomes increasingly critical to your career success, the secretarial crunch intensifies. The situation has reached a crisis point: As the growing shortage of qualified secretaries meets increasing demand, it's getting harder and harder for you to find the person you need to accomplish your goals.

Increased Demand and Growing Shortage

Let's talk about statistics. It makes sense that secretaries will be in greater demand as we move more toward a service-producing rather than goods-producing economy. The 1984–85 *Occupational Outlook Handbook* predicts that by 1995, 75 percent of all new jobs will be in service-producing industries. John Naisbitt envisions in his book *Megatrends* that 80 percent of all workers will be in information services by the year 2000. No wonder secretaries are in demand—information services is their game.

The supply of qualified candidates already cannot meet the demand, and all signs indicate the problem is going to get worse before it gets better. The U.S. Bureau of Labor Statistics anticipates approximately 478,000 secretarial job openings each year through the mid-1990s. Only 5 percent, or about 24,000, of these openings will be new positions created by organizational growth. This leaves some 454,000 openings created annually by secretaries who retire or leave the profession for other reasons.

It is projected that *less than half* of expected annual openings will be filled by newly trained candidates entering the profession, *fewer than 20 percent* by graduates of postsecondary secretarial programs.[1] Assuming postsecondary schools turn out cream-of-the-crop, qualified novices, only 90,800 candidates will be entering the market with the kind of solid training a manager would hope to find in a new employee. That leaves 363,200 positions to be filled by candidates with minimal training—at the high school or adult-education level—or no training whatsoever.

What's really scary about these statistics is that they don't even include openings created by secretaries who move from one job to another. So if you lose a good secretary to a better opportunity—and believe me, there's always someone knocking on a good secretary's door with promises of a better life—you can't rely on an influx of new recruits to fill your need. Speaking of new recruits, let's look at the training situation.

What About New Recruits?

What *can* we assume about those coming into the field from postsecondary programs? Private secretarial schools and two-year colleges offering secretarial programs all have the same thing to report: enrollment is down—way down.

At the State University of New York College of Technology at Alfred, N.Y., which in the early 1970s had the reputation for offering one of the most demanding secretarial curriculums in the Northeast, enrollment in the Executive Secretarial Studies program has dropped considerably. In the mid-1970s, the school averaged an enrollment of 180 students, about 100 of whom

[1]Department of Labor, Bureau of Labor Statistics: *Occupational Outlook Handbook*, 1986/87 Edition, Bulletin 25; *Job Futures: An Occupational Outlook to 1992*, 1986/87 Edition.

successfully completed the program. In 1987, there were 65 students enrolled, of whom about 40 graduated.

Some believe enrollment is down simply because there are fewer high-school-age people in general as the baby-boom generation moves into its 30s. But many feel the reasons behind declining enrollment are more complex, involving the women's movement and many of the factors we will be discussing later in this chapter: the low prestige of the job, limited salary potential, and the expected limited opportunity in career growth.

At the same time, demand for graduates is high and competition for new recruits is intense. The Katharine Gibbs School, one of the most well-known and well-respected secretarial schools on the East Coast, boasts an average of *10 job offers per graduate* through its placement office. Gibbs operates 11 schools in the Boston/New York/Washington, D.C., area and reports that that figure is even higher in metropolitan compared to suburban areas.

Alfred State College of Technology reports an interesting new trend in recruiting practices: the temporary agency as a prospective employer. This may reflect the fact that many companies have come to rely on temporary agencies to fill their support staff needs in the common situation where they are unable to fill open positions quickly themselves. And, according to the chairman of the Secretarial Studies Department at Alfred, competition among agencies for new graduates is fierce. If Agency A learns that Agency B has visited the college, Agency A often will make a second visit to try to lure students away from Agency B.

Agencies apparently are not hiring only for their own benefit, either. Alfred sees a major change in recruiting practice as large corporations sign contracts with temporary agencies to handle hiring for them as a means of cutting costs. This way a company can try out a new secretary before deciding whether to keep him or her. This is one way to solve the growing problem of dissatisfaction among secretaries. By working through a temporary agency, the company can turn back to the agency someone who may have what it considers an attitude problem rather than have to deal with it on its own.

Poor attitudes among secretarial students is a common problem. Many schools report that students show very little interest in what they are learning. One school reported it was not unusual to find failing grades for students who were absent 25 or 30 times in a semester or who simply stopped coming to class. An instructor at another school believes that the students don't seem to want to be secretaries—their parents put them in the school because they didn't have anything else to do. Many seem unhappy about the profession before they've even begun.

Officials at many schools claim that the caliber of students in general is not the same as it once was. Their basic skill levels, especially language and writing skills, are not up to snuff. The Katharine Gibbs School reports that more remediation than acceleration must now be provided. Courses that once were offered as a review, such as grammar, are now the first exposure the student receives. Many faculty members believe this phenomenon is not limited to secretarial schools, but is only a part of the larger problem with education in general.

On the other side of the coin, some school officials notice a decline in the technical skill levels of incoming students. This reflects an increased emphasis on academic subjects in secondary schools that bring up educational levels, an emphasis which no longer allows the student time to focus on specialty subjects such as typing and shorthand.

The fact cannot be avoided that students now moving into the secretarial field are not the same as they once were. It's safe to say that high school students graduating in the top of their class are less likely to enroll in secretarial programs than in the past. Few young men at this point tend to enter what is still considered a female-dominated profession, and women are no longer limited to choosing traditionally female-dominated professions.

Other social and economic factors enter into the career decision as well. For most of this country, the days of man as provider and woman as full-time homemaker are gone. The Bureau of Labor Statistics reports that while as recently as the 1950s two-thirds of all families were of the man/breadwinner, woman/homemaker type, this is true in less than one-third of families today. The current economic climate and desired standard of living among Americans in many cases now requires a two-paycheck family.

Working women are no longer merely providing secondary income. But that's precisely how many consider secretarial work—as an interim job, not a career. Secretarial work is certainly not the first profession of choice for the serious career-minded individual.

Other social factors may influence the decision not to choose secretarial work: with the 50 percent and higher divorce rate we live with today, women are afraid of being left to raise families and support themselves. They think a secretarial career will not allow them to do so. The high cost of day care also means that it is not financially worthwhile for many people to work as a secretary.

In any case, the secretarial-training schools are having a hard time providing what is needed by today's organization, not only in terms of quantity, but also quality. There has been a shift in what is most sought after in a prospective secretary as well. While recruiters for a while were most concerned with a candidate's ability to operate automated equipment, Gibbs reports that prospective employers now consider "soft skills"—appearance, pride, and professionalism—almost more important than technical skills because most anyone can be trained to use computers. The Wood Secretarial School of New York City echoes this experience, stating that professionalism is the key concern of recruiting corporations.

Yet, many schools are finding it's harder to instill soft skills like pride and professionalism than it is to teach students about complicated computers. Why? For the same reasons many secretaries are dissatisfied, some are leaving the profession, and others are dissuaded from entering it in the first place, as we'll soon discuss.

Beyond Statistics

There's still one missing piece to this story. Statistics of supply and demand are compelling, yet they don't take into account a major factor in the secretarial crunch: the large number of unhappy secretaries who seek to leave the profession. While we have no accurate measure of how many highly qualified secretaries are dissatisfied, all evidence points to the fact that their numbers are large. The president of one secretarial recruiting firm in New York City has an eye-opening story to tell.

This agency handles strictly high-level secretarial positions, most in the $25,000–$30,000 salary range. Linda reports that she sees a whole stratum of candidates who have no place to turn. These women (as is usually the case) are highly qualified secretaries, usually with 10 or more years' experience, often supervisory, seeking positions that are or will lead to entry-level management jobs. Such candidates don't mind using their secretarial skills. It's not that they refuse to type—they simply want more than what the typical secretarial position offers.

This group is large. Linda says at least one out of three people who contact her agency find they are really displaced. Secretarial agencies such as Linda's have difficulty placing them because such upwardly mobile secretarial positions are extremely hard to come by. Management recruiting firms don't want them because their salary range is below the minimum they handle.

The reality is that entry- or middle-level management positions are filled in most organizations either by new college or MBA graduates or by promotion from within. Secretaries rarely are considered for such promotions, especially those coming from the outside. Many outsiders are there for that very reason. Despite whatever education and experience the secretary may have to offer, it's the same old story: once a secretary, always a secretary.

And, watch out. Some of the enlightened have keyed into this large unhappy segment of the work force and begun a campaign to save the secretary. Numerous books designed to help secretaries break out of the secretarial rut have come out recently. Variations on a theme, these books replay a single message: Managers will not change. The only road to happiness is the one that takes you out of the secretarial profession. Just what you need to make things even worse.

It's not news that a lot of secretaries are unhappy. What is news is that secretaries are rethinking what it means to be a secretary. The handwriting is on the wall—secretaries are changing; managers must change too in order to attract and keep the highly qualified secretaries they need to get the job done.

Whenever there is change, there is disruption before a new equilibrium can be reached. What you need to get through this turbulent time is a little insight into the current state of the secretarial profession as it affects your work life and guidelines for making the relationship work.

You've probably never had training in how to work with a secretary. Somehow a course entitled "Working with a Secretary 101" has yet to make it into college, business, or professional school curricula. Even if you're one of the few lucky managers who have had corporate training along these lines, most likely it was a canned course that didn't take into account the beneath-the-surface realities of this crucial working relationship.

First, the insight. The same factors that create secretarial dissatisfaction affect your ability to work with a secretary to your ultimate advantage. Let's closely examine this.

What Is It with Secretaries Today?

Backlash of the Women's Movement

The feminist movement has had resounding effects on virtually all aspects of our society. Over the past two decades, broad changes in perspective and attitude have had an enormous influence on both the secretarial profession and the secretary/manager relationship. Lynn, a legal secretary for the past 15 years, is a case in point.

When Lynn was a young woman contemplating her future in the 1960s, she told her uncle, a successful attorney, that she wanted to be a lawyer. Her uncle responded, "Oh, you don't want to be a lawyer. Women lawyers are hard and stern. You don't want to be like that. It's not suitable for a nice young woman like you."

Lynn took her uncle's remarks to heart and noticed her desire to be a lawyer didn't get much support from others either. She decided to pursue a legal secretarial career instead. At least this way she'd be in a law environment, she reasoned, a field she thought she would enjoy. A legal secretary at that time was considered an elite secretarial position and was looked upon as having a certain prestige.

How times change. Lynn certainly wouldn't get the same advice today. Young women of the 1980s are being told, "Don't be a secretary, be an executive or a lawyer"—just as they are being told, "Don't be a nurse, be a doctor," or above all, "Don't be just a housewife." The push is on for women to work outside the home and to move into more nontraditional work areas.

There is a definite pink-collar stigma to being a secretary—any kind of secretary. It affects the mindset and behavior of those in the profession, which in turn affects the manager's ability to work successfully in the secretary/manager relationship.

Secretaries and managers alike have adopted an almost unconscious "just a secretary" attitude. The message is clear: It's not okay to be a secretary. Even those who are happy with their work and proud of being secretaries can't help but feel somewhat defensive. It's hard to escape the pervasive attitude that if you actually want to be a secretary, there must be something wrong with you. It's no wonder a general malaise is evident among those in the profession. It's hard to be enthusiastic when no one expects you to be.

The women's movement has stirred up things in other ways as well, as men and women, managers and secretaries search for a new protocol in working together. For one thing, classic male/female, dominant/submissive roles are no longer standard in private lives or in the office, and the helpmate or office wife role of the secretary no longer fits so comfortably, particularly where the manager is a woman.

The women's movement is the most obvious environmental influence on the secretarial profession and the secretary/manager relationship. Yet, it's only the tip of the iceberg.

Secretarial Stereotyping

The stereotyped view of the secretary as a perk of the manager's job, as an unintelligent, unambitious, less-important helping hand, has created enormous barriers to secretary/manager team success. Although the secretarial role has evolved, secretaries continue to be regarded and treated as though they still functioned as the secretary of yesteryear.

High technology has had a huge impact on the role of secretaries. As high-tech equipment was introduced, there was much speculation as to what its effect would be on the secretary. Some feared the secretary would become nothing more than a production worker, expected to churn out more documents than ever. In most cases, high-speed equipment has added dimension to the secretary's role by providing the capability to complete paper-work more quickly, thus allowing the secretary to take on more administrative and creative responsibilities. It's now evident that the automated office has not spelled the demise of the secretary, but in fact only brought to light what has really been true all along: Secretaries do a lot more than type.

It will take time for the awareness of this realistic view of the secretary to spread. Lynn's continuing saga gives a picture of what most secretaries today are up against.

After completing a two-year college program in Legal Secretarial Science, Lynn landed her first job at a large law firm. After three months on the job, Lynn was up for her first perfor-mance review. Andrew, one of the attorneys in the department, conducted the interview.

"Lynn, we're extremely pleased with your performance so far and are very happy to have you with us. But you're so bright— you seem too smart to be a secretary. Are you sure that's what you want to be?"

Talk about a mixed message. Lynn wasn't sure whether she was being complimented or insulted. Lynn felt pleased to hear she was doing so well but somehow guilty at the same time. She got the underlying message: Being a secretary means you're not smart or if you really *are* smart, you wouldn't be a secretary.

On the up side, at least Andrew wasn't so blinded by an assumption that secretaries aren't smart that he overlooked Lynn's intelligence. But would it affect how she would be utilized on the job? This question remained unanswered.

For the time being, Lynn shrugged off the probably unin-tended slur because the praise made her feel worthy and especially because of the solid raise that went along with the review. She was confident that continued high performance would gain her the career advancement she desired, in terms of both more money and responsibility.

Two years later, Lynn held the same position at the law firm. A valued member of the department, Lynn obtained substan-tial salary increases over that time. The content of her job, however, remained the same. Despite the fact that the attorneys seemed aware of Lynn's above-average intelligence, they continued to rely most heavily on her technical skills, such as typing, filing, copying, and collating. After all, isn't that what a secretary is supposed to do? Lynn craved more meat to her work, but didn't know quite how to go about taking on more responsibility. Of course, the attorneys didn't offer any ideas along those lines.

The stereotype was at work on both sides. Lynn seemed to plug along waiting for someone else to save her from growing boredom. Andrew and his colleagues probably didn't even notice that anything was wrong with the status quo. It's a reflection of the kind of underutilization secretaries have long complained of and an example of how managers can be blindly directed by stereotype assumptions.

Here is a summary of assumptions you must identify within yourself and abandon for your own good:

☐ *Secretaries lack ability.* They aren't capable of doing anything better than secretarial work.

☐ *Secretaries lack motivation.* They aren't interested in doing anything better than secretarial work.

☐ *Secretaries are not promotable.* They don't belong to the organizational pool of talent—they are are separate and apart from the rest of the staff.

☐ *Secretaries aren't career-oriented.* Secretarial work is a dead end; therefore, secretaries are people who don't care about getting ahead.

☐ *All secretaries are equal.* Secretarial work consists largely of typing, filing, and answering the telephone.

By holding to an outmoded view of the secretarial role, you lose out on the immense potential of the secretary as a value-added assistant. Worse, you may well find it difficult to keep a secretary—especially that rare professional.

The Perception Gap

Bosses cannot take total blame for managing secretaries non-productively. Traditional organizational handling of secretaries also has a lot to do with the problems secretaries and managers face today.

Most people agree that if all the secretaries in an office left at lunch and didn't return, operations would come to a halt. Yet, historically, secretaries have not been accepted as full-fledged members of an organization. How the secretarial function is perceived compared to its actual responsibilities and the difficulty in coming up with a quantifiable measure of how a secretary contributes to company goals distort a secretary's actual value to an organization. And management's treatment of the company's support staff often reflects this perception gap.

In the past, secretaries were assigned to managers as a perk, rather than as functioning team members. While this may no longer be a usual practice, attitudes toward secretaries as mere window dressing unfortunately prevail. Secretaries have long been considered a separate stratum—not part of a company's talent pool—and traditionally have received different treatment from other staff members in terms of rules, regulations, and benefits.

Although they work closely with management, secretaries are often treated more like blue-collar workers than the true professionals they are. Most secretaries are paid hourly rather than by salary and are labeled "nonexempt." This even *sounds* negative. Many secretaries, not understanding the meaning of the term, strive for promotions to exempt positions, longing to belong to the elite. They are surprised to find it merely means they are no longer entitled to overtime pay!

Company policies that concern secretarial compensation often raise many problems. Secretaries complain that although they may work late or through lunch without claiming overtime, they are allowed little, if any, flexibility in time away from the office, and may even be called to task for coming in a few minutes late in the morning.

One company found itself in serious trouble with its secretaries over a policy stating that managers who worked through lunch were allowed to order something to eat at the company's expense, while secretaries who worked right alongside those managers were not. The secretaries felt like they were not good enough to be given lunch.

It's true that federal compensation laws in some cases direct how companies must administer compensation and overtime, but not all secretarial positions in question are properly classified as nonexempt. Taking into account what is actually done on the job, many secretarial positions might well be found to fall outside these requirements. But more about what secretaries really do later. For now, the point is that whether required by law or not, these kinds of practices have a negative effect on a secretary's attitude.

One area of difficulty that cannot be blamed on any higher authority is the way secretarial salaries are determined. A secretary's pay usually is not commensurate with the actual duties performed or the level of responsibility assumed, but rather is tied to the level of the manager to whom he or she reports. Education and experience do not necessarily lead to secretarial pay increases. And, because many organizations do not recognize a career path of the profession or otherwise distinguish among secretarial positions, salary spreads are limited. The secretary who takes the initiative and attempts to negotiate for an appropriate salary by proving it has been earned commonly meets with the response: "We can't give it to you because then all the other secretaries will want it too."

This brings us back to a misperception alluded to earlier: All secretaries are assumed equal. Organizations have traditionally considered secretaries categorically rather than individually. No differentiation among secretarial positions in terms of titles or job descriptions is the rule rather than the exception in most organizations. At best, organizations use broad categories to distinguish groups of secretaries that share a salary level, such as Secretary I, Secretary II, Secretary III. Even in such cases, salaries again are based not on the actual requirements of the position, but on the level of manager to whom the secretary is assigned.

Job descriptions for support-staff positions rarely exist. Even when job descriptions are used, more often than not they are inaccurate by failing to reflect the true depth of the position. Again, overemphasizing the typical technical aspects of a secretary's function means little, if any, attention is given to the aspects of each secretary's unique position in the department and with the manager(s) with whom the secretary works. It's no wonder secretaries feel overlooked and less important.

Even by focusing on the technical aspects of the secretary's function, it's hard to ignore the fact that secretarial positions are not all alike. Word processing and computers are used in different companies in diverse configurations. Some companies use a centralized word-processing center with electronic typewriters at each secretary's desk. Others work with a centralized system with satellite equipment at each secretarial workstation so that secretaries can communicate with the main center. The most progressive offices install computers not only at support-staff desks, but in managers' offices as well. Work is initiated directly on the computer, allowing managers and secretaries immediate interaction. The fact that each office configuration and, therefore, secretarial utilization is different illustrates contemporary reality: There is no one clear-cut definition of the secretary.

Secretaries are dealt with in subtle ways that reflect outmoded assumptions. They have effectively been kept to the sidelines, expected to be seen and not heard. Secretaries generally aren't kept informed of the goals and activities of the companies or departments in which they work. More often than not they are left out of staff meetings, even though what goes on behind closed doors has much to do with their daily work. Apparently it's assumed that secretaries don't need to know, don't want to know, or even worse, aren't capable of understanding what's going on around them. In short, secretaries have long been treated as though they weren't real members of the organizational team. Being continually left out leaves secretaries feeling like second-class citizens in their own companies.

Most people consider secretarial work a dead end. If this is true, it's only because organizations keep it that way. Most companies don't bother with career planning for secretaries since secretarial jobs are not traditionally viewed as long-term, career positions. There are no clear-cut career paths for the secretary who wishes to climb from an entry-level position to more challenging assignments. The most a secretary can strive for is to tag along as a manager gets promoted or to move up and work for other higher-level managers. Even then, such opportunities for advancement are not clearly set out. Secretarial positions do not, of course, appear on organization charts.

As already pointed out, management has been slow to recognize that secretaries have more to offer than just filling interim positions. Upward mobility into nonsecretarial positions is the exception to the rule. An invisible but definite barrier has kept secretaries in their place—and this has a lot to do with secretarial dissatisfaction. The conclusion of Lynn's story is illustrative.

Three years into the job, Lynn remained content, learning all about functioning in a large organization and her particular field of law. But she craved more challenge. When a position for a paralegal opened up in the department, Lynn was very excited about it. After all, she had been around for a while and had learned a lot about the inner workings of the department, to say nothing of how the attorneys liked things done. Further, Lynn was familiar with this particular area of the law and had built up a solid knowledge of court procedures. Her two-year college education was a bonus when added to her extensive experience. She applied for the job, confident she would be the department's first choice. After all, hadn't Andrew himself said that Lynn was too smart to be just a secretary?

What a surprise. Lynn wasn't chosen for the position. In fact, she wasn't even considered for it. Why not? Officially, because of a company policy that stated that a bachelor's degree was required of paralegals. Lynn couldn't believe her ears. She knew for a fact that exceptions to policy were routinely made when senior partners deemed it appropriate, and further, she knew of a recent similar situation where an exception had been made.

The real story came down some time later through an unofficial communication from one attorney who, feeling badly for Lynn, believed she deserved the truth. Apparently, the powers that be felt that being a good secretary didn't mean a person could be good at anything else. Their evidence was the similar situation that Lynn had remembered. That secretary who was promoted was unable to perform the new required duties. Management also feared that if secretaries were routinely promoted to other positions, the firm would lose all its good secretaries.

Add it all up: Secretaries lack ability, secretaries are all alike, secretaries are not promotable. The result of this kind of illogical thinking causes a company to lose the valuable contributions a secretary may have to offer and also demoralizes every secretary in the organization. The knowledge that no matter how high your performance, you'll always stay in the same job fosters a "what's the use" attitude among the support staff. Is it any wonder some secretaries have negative attitudes?

It may seem that many of the problems we've discussed are beyond your control as an individual manager. Later chapters will discuss these issues further and provide suggestions for how you might work around them. But for now realize that if your reply to secretarial dissatisfaction is, "That's the way it is, there's nothing I can do about it," a secretary may well take your words to mean, "I don't *care* to do anything about it," or, worse, "I agree with the policy." Here's where you can really run into trouble.

The Coffee-Klatch Syndrome

A big obstacle to secretary/manager team success resulting directly from organizational mismanagement of secretaries is worthy of discussion. I call it the coffee-klatch syndrome. Secretaries who feel isolated and powerless to change working conditions tend to form solid support groups among themselves. Pressure is strong within these informal groups to conform to unspoken standards of behavior, with the threat of being ostracized keeping members in line. It works. If secretaries are banished from their own informal peer group and aren't welcomed into other staff circles, where else have they to turn?

While a primary purpose of the coffee klatch is to meet the social needs of secretaries, it also serves another purpose. It is the vehicle through which the support staff retaliates, although indirectly, against management practices considered unfair and against managers who are perceived to treat secretaries in an unacceptable fashion.

The coffee klatch often is directly responsible for establishing negative norms among secretaries, such as a general uncooperative attitude toward the enemy (management and managers). An us-versus-them mindset is fostered. Let's face it, you're one of "them" unless you take positive steps to bridge the secretary/management gap.

More specifically, the coffee klatch influences performance standards. Behavior patterns develop, some harmless, others not so harmless, that reflect secretaries' reaction to management practices and policies. Where the secretary/management relationship in a company is healthy, this is not a problem; unfortunately, that's more the exception than the rule. Negative behaviors often reflect an attempt to take control in one situation where there is no control over another condition. Coffee-klatch behaviors are obvious symptoms of serious underlying problems that usually revolve around one basic flaw in the company: a lack of communication between support staff and management.

For example, it is an unspoken rule among secretaries in one company that lunch hour be stretched to at least one hour and ten minutes. A secretary who actually returns on time at the one-hour mark is frowned upon by the peer group. Within the same group, it is expected behavior in conjunction with this lunch rule to sign the time sheet to cover for those extra few minutes. If a secretary chooses not to go along and signs in 1:10 P.M. at 1:10 P.M. instead of 1:00 P.M. at 1:10 P.M., that secretary would cause a real problem, since everyone returning afterwards would also have to sign in accurately. It's difficult to stand alone against the group because the klatch holds a grudge against any secretary who refuses to conform.

This norm reflects secretarial resistance to having to sign in and out in the first place. The attitude is, "After all, managers don't have to sign a time sheet, why should I?" Or, "Managers go to lunch whenever they please; it's more efficient if I go to lunch at the same time as my manager does. Besides, sometimes I might need to go earlier or later than just between 12:00 P.M. and 1:00 P.M.. And managers stay out as long as they please. Why should I be limited to precisely one hour? After all, I often come in a few minutes early in the morning and stay a few minutes late at the end of the day. It all balances out." No one was interested in how the secretaries felt about rules concerning lunch hour, so the coffee klatch took over and substituted its own rules to compensate.

Another company went to great expense to improve the efficiency of its support operations and enhance the working conditions of its support staff only to see its efforts backfire. All new equipment was ordered—sophisticated telephone system, state-of-the-art dictating equipment, and word-processing equipment for every workstation. Ironically, while the intent was to foster greater cooperation, management's actions instead intensified secretaries' feelings of isolation and widened the gap between the support staff and management.

The first problem arose when the secretaries, the very people who would utilize the equipment, were not included in the selection process. They were not even asked what features would be most helpful, even though it should have been obvious that the secretaries themselves knew best what they needed to accomplish their work goals.

The secretaries were offended by being left out of decisions that obviously directly affected their own work life. They talked about it with managers who would listen but more among themselves, since not too many managers were interested. This reinforced the group's negative attitude toward management and the purchases, which were meant to improve working conditions, not deteriorate them.

The equipment arrived and was presented to the secretaries along with a set of policies to accompany implementation of the new office configuration. The new workstations were designed to provide continuous support coverage to managers in each department. Management directed that secretaries were never to leave the department unattended; if one secretary were away from the desk, another secretary had to be told in order to cover in his or her absence. Lunch hours were to be coordinated so that one secretary remained in the department at all times. The secretary who was covering the lunch period was not only responsible for answering all phones, but also for assisting any manager assigned in the department who needed help during that time.

Enormous problems resulted. Not only were the secretaries resistant to the new equipment, they were resentful about the new rules they felt were dumped on them. Some departments simply ignored the rule concerning lunch coverage. Others followed policy only as it suited their plans, claiming unusual circumstances the rest of the time. Some of those who complied and stayed through the regular lunch hour neglected to answer the phones or refused to help a manager, replying, "I'm too busy."

More problems than benefits were created by the new policies. Incredible time and energy were expended by supervisors and administrative staff in attempting to enforce policy and in constant reminders to the support staff about correct procedures. Obviously, cooperation cannot be mandated; it must be nurtured.

Individual managers suffered the real brunt of the secretaries' resistance. Managers' phones would not be answered when they were away from their desks and if an emergency came up during that lunch hour, they often could not find a secretary to help. If no secretaries were available in one department, a manager would run to another only to be turned away, often rudely at that.

This brings us to the most dangerous element of the coffee klatch as it concerns you, the individual manager. The group will blackball a manager who has proven unworthy of its support. Depending on the crime, a manager can find himself or herself completely without effective secretarial support.

Take Tom, for instance, commonly known in his company as "the boy who cried wolf." Tom is a classic workaholic. He doesn't walk down the hall, he runs. He always has more projects in the works than anyone else and, despite his less-than-graceful style, is usually successful in seeing them through to completion. He's a sort of walking whirlwind and his office reflects it. Papers are everywhere, covering every horizontal surface, including much of the floor.

Tom has had difficulty keeping secretaries—he's been through three this past year. Even when there is a secretary assigned to him, he always seems to have too much work for him or her to handle. When that happens, which is frequently, Tom runs down the hall to find another secretary to help him. He always says, "Please help me. I've got this super rush job and my secretary can't do it." Although it was a rush to Tom because he couldn't wait to get it done, many times the project wasn't really a rush as the accepted meaning of the term implies, namely, "it must go out today." Secretaries who had done something for Tom, putting their own work aside, would find the same document sitting on his desk two days later. Word spread about Tom. It got to the point where none of the secretaries believed a word he said. In their minds, *nothing* of

Tom's was a rush. The group decided he was *out*. Not only could Tom not get help from other secretaries, he soon found that many of the in-house temporaries refused to work with him either. This became a serious problem when his own permanent secretary resigned and it took two months to find a replacement.

The coffee-klatch syndrome wreaks havoc in many a company. If upper management recognizes secretarial noncooperation as a symptom of underlying difficulties, rarely does it seek to get to the root of problem situations. Unless lines of communication are opened, the gap between secretaries and management only widens. We'll talk more about communication in Chapter 4. For now, realize that you may well be up against a problem in your company that's bigger than both you and your secretary.

If you work in a company with a strong, negatively motivated coffee klatch, it will be up to you to develop a relationship with your secretary that will override the influence of that peer group. The good news is that what matters most to a secretary is how he or she is treated by individual managers. As you read on, you will learn how to rise above whatever organizational ills your secretary suffers.

What It All Means to You

It should be clear by now that there's a problem and that the problem is yours. Statistics tell the big story. You are living the smaller picture, perhaps with a secretary who is less than satisfactory or with a terrific secretary you fear will leave you. The dread you feel about searching for a new secretary is real. It's a seller's market—secretaries have the luxury of choosing for whom they will work. It's up to you to make sure the secretary you need will choose you.

That's part one of your challenge. Part two has to do with successfully managing the secretary/manager relationship and taking best advantage of the potential of that relationship for the benefit of your own career.

Your Secretary—Your Work—Your Career

You realize that a good secretary makes the difference between a pleasant workday and a daily nightmare. But did you ever stop to think about how a secretary can affect the successful completion of your work goals and, in fact, your career climb?

Although secretaries generally have little legitimate authority within an organization, they exercise real influence in several ways. Whether your secretary will choose to act to your advantage or disadvantage depends on the overall quality of your relationship. It's important to be aware of how you are vulnerable and why it's so important to build and maintain a mutually satisfactory work relationship with your secretary.

The most obvious source of a secretary's power is control over your work product. You must rely on a secretary to hold up one end of your work responsibilities, yet your secretary alone determines how quickly work will get done and the quality of that work. This aspect of the secretary's hold on a manager is intensified in the case of those who must share a secretary with one or more other managers.

The secretary's most significant source of power is the information he or she comes to acquire on the job. Secretaries are in a position to gather and disseminate, withhold or share a wealth of information that can bear heavily on your job and career.

Let's start with the most obvious. The secretary is usually the first to see your mail. Your secretary also may screen your phone calls. It's up to your secretary how much information will be passed on or screened out before it reaches you. Information sabotage need not be malicious; some secretaries are just not motivated enough to care whether they help or hurt a boss.

A secretary's access to information goes well beyond papers that cross a desk or words that travel over a telephone line. Because of the secretary's role and also because he or she is usually situated out in the open in an office, a secretary is privy to all kinds of valuable information that can benefit or harm a manager.

Although secretaries are officially left out of the formal communication chain of an organization, they are linking pins or major hubs in the *in*formal communication network of a company. As key players in an organization's informal communication chain, secretaries often hear others in the company talking about you or your department, or about matters that affect you or your department. How secretaries choose to participate in this exchange of information largely depends on the relationship they share with their managers. A secretary can pass information along or ignore what is heard. A secretary can add information to the grapevine— perhaps your secrets or disparaging remarks —or simply choose not to correct whatever inaccuracies are heard. It all depends on how the two of you are working together.

Another source of a secretary's power is public relations, both inside and outside the company. A secretary represents a boss and a company on the job and off. Naturally, how a secretary talks about you and your company when you're not around is of great significance. Again, how a boss and company are portrayed by a secretary depends on the secretary's experience on the job.

Don't underestimate the amount of influence your secretary can wield over your fate. On the up side, in the successful secretary/manager relationship, these sources of secretarial power can be put to use for your definite advantage. You can gain an important edge in climbing that ladder of success by winning over your secretary as an ally and utilizing his or her full range of talents and abilities, including the power sources we've just discussed.

Take It from Here

Essentially, today's secretary/manager experience is based on the influence of a time gone by and what the future requires. Attitudes toward the secretarial profession and the secretary's role need to catch up with the reality of what is needed by today's manager. An enhanced image of the profession is necessary to turn the tide, and it starts with you. It's your challenge to find a secretary who meets your needs and to build a successful, mutually beneficial secretary/manager relationship despite these difficult times. The following chapters will help you do just that.

CHAPTER
TWO

FINDING THE
BEST SECRETARIES

Just how hard is it to find a good secretary? Some argue that there really is no shortage. A head count might indicate that, technically, there are enough to go around. But we're talking about finding you a secretary who's top-notch, not just in terms of skills, but also intelligence, initiative, and motivation—someone who can really help you get ahead in your career. This is where the difficulty lies, for the real professional is in short supply, hard to find, and not easily snared. There are a lot of *secretaries* out there, certainly. The problem is that broad use of this title allows for confusion over its definition. As a result, there is a wide range of competency levels among those wearing the label. As the term is currently used, *secretary* can be someone who has just finished an eight-week correspondence course as well as the seasoned professional who holds a bachelor's degree and a CPS® rating.[1] In practice, many people who call themselves secretaries really don't fit the bill in today's marketplace.

Despite the professional secretary's attempts to battle long-standing stereotypes, many secretaries who feel defeated by long-time treatment as second-class corporate citizens have accepted the stereotype. This type clings to an adversarial mindset, reflects an unprofessional image, possesses an "it's just a job" attitude, and generally does as little as possible to get by on a day-to-day basis—to the detriment of the good name of the profession.

Yes, there are more than enough gum-chewing, clock-watching, underqualified secretaries to go around. Employment agencies can easily waste your time with a parade of candidates that just don't pass muster. Truly career-oriented, highly motivated, competent professionals are in short supply and high demand.

When we talk about finding you a secretary, we're not talking about a simple selection process, because selection implies a choice from among an ample supply of candidates. What you're really

---

[1]Certified Professional Secretary® is a distinction awarded by the Institute for Certifying Secretaries, a department of Professional Secretaries International® (PSI®). Holders of the CPS® rating have met certain education and work experience requirements and passed a two-day, six-part examination measuring secretarial proficiency.

doing is recruiting. Your search, therefore, takes on an important dual marketing aspect: marketing you as a desirable manager with whom to work and marketing the position you have to offer as one that will be attractive to the high-caliber secretary. Of course, not every top-notch secretary you encounter will be right for you. So the process also includes a screening component designed to help you choose not just a competent secretary, but the secretary who is best *for you.*

Using the insight you gained in Chapter 1, you can gain an edge in attracting a good secretary by positioning yourself as top contender for the title "good boss." The contemporary secretary seeks the manager who shares an enlightened view.

Highly qualified secretaries will not stand for being underutilized or undervalued. The contemporary secretary wants an active, productive role for the benefit of the boss, the department, and the organization, but also for the secretary's own career growth. Competent professionals resent being considered a part of the office equipment. They expect to be regarded and treated as significant members of the organizational team.

Abandon any worn-out notions you hold and adopt a progressive set of beliefs concerning the secretary:

□ A secretary is an ally, an assistant to a boss, and a significant team member.

□ A secretary is not just a secretary, but a key staff member with valuable skills.

□ A secretary's skills consist of more than typing and shorthand and should be utilized to their fullest extent.

□ A secretary wants and deserves a career-building job.

□ Secretaries should be regarded as full-fledged members of the corporate team.

□ All secretaries are not alike.

As you take on this progressive perspective, you take your first big step toward finding a secretary who can be a real asset. Let's face it, you need all the help you can get to succeed in today's competitive business environment.

Getting Ready for the Search

When a manager needs a secretary, it is usually a matter of urgency. The recruitment process is ruled by a sense of, "I must get a secretary *immediately.*" It's ironic—while managers are frantic without a secretary, they often give less thought to what to look for in a secretary than they do in choosing where to have lunch. You didn't get where you are by jumping into situations without first properly preparing yourself. The same thoughtful deliberation that goes into other important decisions must go into the recruitment process.

Searching for someone to serve as the other half of a work team is, of course, much more involved than looking for a typist. Further, choosing the right secretary is more critical and complex than selecting any other staff member, because your secretary works more closely with you than any other member of your team.

Preparation for the actual search requires developing a composite of the ideal. You need a list of as many adjectives as you can come up with to describe what you need in a secretary above and beyond mere questions of technical abilities. To imagine your ideal secretary, you need a clear understanding of these factors:

- ☐ Your work style.
- ☐ The nature of your work.
- ☐ The job you have to offer.
- ☐ The work setting.
- ☐ The organizational setting.

Your lists will not only help you screen candidates but ensure that you, the job, your company, and a candidate are all suited to one another. Your outlines will further sell the right candidate, once you've found him or her, on taking the job. You should be as specific as possible in bringing all crucial aspects of each part of the whole out in the open at the outset, leaving nothing to chance.

A secretary who best completes your team is a secretary who complements your strengths and fills in for your weaknesses. Keep this in mind as you work on your lists. Also think about where you are in the scheme of your career: what your goals are and what you need to achieve them. Choose a secretary who can help you achieve those goals.

About You and How You Work

As you attempt to describe yourself, it's helpful to get the candid opinions of others. It's only human to have a hard time seeing yourself objectively, but distorted perceptions about your personality or work style won't help you hire the right secretary.

Avoid using overly general terms. If you have a reputation as a difficult boss, pin down just what *difficult* means. Are you a procrastinator, a perfectionist, or have secretaries considered you unapproachable? Difficult could merely mean you expect a lot of your secretary and just have yet to work with one who appreciates you. Now's your chance to set the record straight and hire a secretary who will thrive on your team because he or she is well suited to it.

Your Work Style

Pinpointing your work style is crucial to hiring a secretary who is compatible with you and will be of most value. Mistakes are commonly made in secretary/manager matching either because managers are unaware of their style or because they assume it's up to the secretary to adjust. A person's working style is not easily changed. A secretary and manager work too closely together to have incompatible work styles.

Ideally, your work style and that of your secretary should complement one another where appropriate. You can gain a lot of help and eliminate a lot of anxiety by creating a situation where your secretary picks up your slack. If you're notably disorganized, for example, hire a secretary who can keep you on track.

To account for any discrepancy between the way you work and the way you think you work, seek out objective opinions. The following should get you thinking.

When are you most productive? Are you a morning, afternoon, or evening person? If you do your best work two hours before everyone else arrives, you'll need a secretary who's also a morning person. If you tend not to get moving until 4:00 in the afternoon, it helps to have a self-starting secretary who can be productive without you leading the way all day. If you're the type who gets most of the work done after everyone else has gone home, you'll either need a secretary who doesn't mind frequently working overtime or who doesn't mind facing a pile of work on his or her desk first thing every morning.

Compare your attitude concerning work versus leisure time with that of the prospective secretary. Do you lean more toward the style of a workaholic or a good-time Charlie? Consider your expectations of how hard someone should work. Do you think people should be busy every minute of an eight-hour day or do you expect breaks now and then? What is your attitude toward lunch hour? Some people skip lunch without a thought while others feel lunch is an inalienable right. What is your attitude toward overtime? Some feel it is an imposition while others take it for granted. Some expect overtime on short notice while others need to plan for it well in advance.

What is your career versus personal life orientation? Find a secretary whose attitude toward the work and family balance matches yours. Which comes first and how much weight and priority do you give to each? For one person, missing a son's baseball game to work overtime is a matter of course, while to another, family comes first no matter what. What is your reaction to time off for family emergencies or just plain family business?

If you are a perfectionist, you will need a secretary who is, too. Otherwise, it will drive a secretary crazy when you revise a letter four times or drive you crazy when a letter has to be retyped four times because it's not set up just so. If you're not a stickler for detail, don't hire a secretary who is—unless you need someone to cover for your bad spelling and grammar. Perfectionists tend to spend more time on projects than nonperfectionists would like, which can create friction.

No one likes to admit to being a procrastinator, but let's face it, many of us put off the difficult jobs until the eleventh hour. Or, to put it in more positive terms, some people produce better under pressure. The procrastinator can drive a secretary up a wall. If you tend toward this style, admit it. What's important is that a secretary understand this about you at the outset and agree to put up with it. You can point out your redeeming qualities to make up for it. Many secretaries put up with the procrastinator in return for other concessions. For example, the secretary who accepts your last-minute emergencies without complaint may appreciate occasional long lunches during slack time for running personal errands. If you are serious about overcoming this habit, find a secretary who is an excellent time manager and assertive enough to keep on your back about not putting off important projects.

A big question is your delegating style. How much control are you willing to relinquish to your secretary? Do you mind if your secretary edits your work or do you welcome the help? Are you one to watch over a secretary's shoulder or are you comfortable to leave him or her alone? Do you expect your secretary to remind you of things that need to be done or do you keep track and do the reminding? Are you away from the office a good bit of the time, relying heavily on a secretary to get things done in your absence, or do you prefer to handle things yourself from a distance?

What is your work style under pressure? Do you tend to hide and want to be left alone? Or do you want someone to keep you company through difficult periods? Are you a screamer or the silent type when things get rough? Do you work on one thing at a time and see it through to completion or juggle many projects as you feel inspired? Do you work by the book or are you more the operator type who enjoys moving in and around the system?

Personality Blending

When considering personality, keep two points in mind: how a secretary's personality suits your own and how it fits the job.

Finding a secretary whose personality meshes with yours is a tricky business. When it comes to overall personality blending, you may choose to follow either an "opposites attract" or "birds of a feather" philosophy. You will notice as you add adjectives to your list that, as with work styles, some traits are better matched similarly, others complementarily. For example, two moody people tend to be explosive; if you're the moody type, you'll want a secretary who is particularly even tempered and able to roll with the punches. In some cases it's better for you and your secretary to be alike: For instance, if you're a stickler for businesslike formalities, a secretary who yells down the hall for you will drive you crazy. Also look for personality traits you wish you had and seek to fill that lack with your secretary. Here are some traits to get you thinking. Do people consider you:

- ☐ Shy or outgoing?
- ☐ Open or private?
- ☐ Serious or fun loving?
- ☐ Talkative or quiet?
- ☐ Outspoken or reserved?
- ☐ Sensitive or aloof?
- ☐ Businesslike or casual?
- ☐ Disciplined or carefree?
- ☐ Rigid or flexible?
- ☐ Moody or even tempered?
- ☐ Energetic or laid back?
- ☐ Uptight or easygoing?

What's most important is that you hire a secretary who complements you in ways that will help you accomplish your work goals and get ahead in your career. For example, manager Susan supervised 10 staff members. Susan was a very private person who found it hard to make the kind of casual small talk her subordinates seemed to crave. There was tension between Susan and her staff that made it difficult for Susan to cultivate the team effort she needed to accomplish work goals. The workers in fact took offense at Susan's apparent standoffishness and felt she thought she was somehow better than them.

Susan wisely hired a secretary with an open friendliness and knack for remembering personal details about people — goings-on at home, outside interests, and so on. Susan's secretary, Jane, took on the role of social ambassador on Susan's behalf. As Susan's intermediary, Jane kept up the personalized end of Susan's relationships with her subordinates. Jane would point out to Susan important happenings in staff members' lives and would kick off casual conversations as individuals were coming and going from her office so that Susan could express an appropriate interest, an interest she felt but just had difficulty expressing on her own.

You also must consider the nature of your work and the personality a secretary needs to succeed in the position. Is your work sales oriented? Think of sales in a broad sense. Will your secretary be called on to promote you or your work, service, or product to others in person or on the telephone?

Think about whether the secretarial position is a social one. Will your secretary need to interact with many others or be more of a loner? Will you and your secretary work as a part of a larger departmental team or more as a solo team within your organization?

Consider the pace of your work. Is it fast, consistent, cyclical, or unpredictable? A legal secretary to a labor attorney, for example, must be comfortable working in a chaotic environment where emergency situations may give rise to heavy work loads on a moment's notice. Another legal secretary working with a real estate attorney may have the leisure of preparing for closings well in advance of closing dates.

The Work Scene

Many factors in the work setting directly affect a secretary's work efforts. The more specific you can be, the better you prepare a prospective secretary for what it would be like to work with you. You should also, of course, point out the positive aspects of the work setting from a secretary's point of view for marketing purposes. Don't try to hide the negatives, however; surprises only lead to problems later.

Let's take a look at your work setting—first the small picture. Think about how you and your secretary fit into the immediate physical and social surroundings:

□ Do you work alone or as part of a larger team?

□ How much interaction is there among you and your coworkers? How often will your secretary have to deal with these or other people?

□ What kind of people are they? Is it a serious or fun-loving group? Do they tend to be critical and competitive or is it all for one and one for all?

□ How do people in the department treat newcomers? Is there an initation rite for new employees before acceptance by the group?

□ Do fellow workers pitch in to help each other out?

□ Will others help train your secretary? Will he or she rely solely on you or have to fend for himself or herself?

□ Do higher-ups work nearby or do they tend to stay away?

□ Will you share your secretary with one or more other managers? Will any of your subordinates need the secretary's help as well? How many people will the secretary unofficially support?

What about the physical setting in which you work:

□ Will your secretary sit out in the open or in some sort of closed cubicle?

□ How much room will the secretary have? Are files maintained at the secretary's workstation?

□ How close is the secretary's station to your office and the offices of others to whom he or she will report? What kind of communication system will be used?

□ Where are support services located in relation to his or her workstation, such as the copying center and satellite copiers, mail center, receptionist or message center, travel center, or any other areas of the building needed to accomplish daily work?

□ How many people share the copy machine and other support services?

The physical work setting is of great importance to a secretary. Be sensitive to the fact that secretaries don't enjoy sitting out in the open, as is often the case. If your secretary will work in some kind of enclosure or in an office, by some rare chance, this is a very positive point for you to present. And, of course, the more room a secretary has, the better. If your secretary will not be enclosed or semienclosed, maybe there's something you can do to create an illusion of privacy. Perhaps some large plants around the station would help or you could situate the desk in such a manner as to give the station an air of privacy. Expressing your awareness of the issue is a step in the right direction in any event.

The availability, proximity, and effectiveness of support services is important. A secretary needs to anticipate how much running around will be required during the day to get the job done.

Your Company's Culture

Now think about the bigger picture—the organizational setting. You want a secretary who will thrive in the corporate culture of your organization. An organization's culture produces a certain value system as well as norms of behavior to which your secretary must be comfortable adhering.

Attach as many specific descriptive labels to your organization as possible, such as laid back, staid, conservative, high risk, fast paced, constantly changing, high pressure, bureaucratic, or growing. For instance, Xerox Corporation sums up its corporate culture by stating this characteristic required of the Xerox employee: "The willingness to be part of the Xerox challenge: ability to handle changing priorities and adjust to a quick-turn-around environment."

What values are shared and accepted by employees in your company? Some organizations value conformity, others foster innovation and creativity. Employees feel fortunate just to work for some companies. It is understood that the company does a lot for the employees and the employees, therefore, give the company all they've got if they want to stay on. Some organizations foster feelings of security, motivating employees by offering attractive retirement packages. An applicant's background will have a lot to do with how well he or she will fit into your organization.

Many secretaries are unaware of how the culture, rules, and unofficial practices of organizations of various sizes and configurations affect daily work life. Make sure you let a candidate know full well what he or she is in for to avoid serious difficulty later. Undoubtedly, there is a certain way of getting things done in your company. Think of the many unwritten rules you live by in your company and put them on paper. A candidate must know full well what he or she is getting into before accepting a job.

Let's look at a disastrous situation where a highly qualified secretary was hired for a position with no understanding of what the organizational situation would be.

Angela was a top-notch secretary with an associate's degree and five solid years' experience behind her. She had never worked in a corporate environment and when moving to a new city decided to give the large company a try. An intelligent woman with excellent technical skills, Angela was quickly hired to fill a middle-level secretarial slot working for five managers: one principal manager and the four who reported to him. She was told it was a very busy position, which Angela approved of because she enjoyed a quick-paced environment.

She was totally unprepared, however, for the red tape that would slow her efforts in accomplishing a heavy work load, such as rules governing such simple matters as sending out letters. Accustomed to simply mailing a letter once it was signed by a manager, Angela now found that letters going to anyone outside of the corporate headquarters in which she worked required the approval of 11 managers other than those to whom she reported. The official process required filling out and attaching a certain form and forwarding the letter through interoffice mail until it returned with all required signatures. After several weeks of frustration over letters taking forever to come back, or worse, getting lost or buried on someone's desk somewhere along the line, Angela finally picked up the fact that common practice is to personally walk a letter through the approval process. Angela was not the type of person who enjoyed finding ways to work around the system. She stuck it out long enough to earn vacation time and then left for a spot in a much smaller company.

What Kind of Secretary Do You Need?

Think about each of the foregoing considerations (you may find it helpful to refer to the checklist/worksheet on page 45) and make careful notes of what applies to your situation. Again, the more specific you can be, the better. Next we'll look at what secretaries have to offer. Bearing your lists in mind, match specific secretarial traits to your identified needs to further prepare a composite of your ideal secretary.

Evaluating Secretarial Skills

Technical Skills—The Basics

Let's talk about secretarial skills or, to be more specific, technical skills. You need to be sure a candidate has the technical abilities you require. Make sure, however, that the tests used will tell you what you need to know.

Most secretaries are incorrectly judged first and foremost by typing speed and accuracy. How often have you heard from a personnel counselor, "I've got a great candidate—80 words per minute with no errors. Then there's another one who tested 85 words per minute but with five errors." It's ridiculous to assign such weight to standard typing tests, first of all because there is more to a secretary's job than how quickly letters are typed. Further, since most offices today use electronic typewriters, word processors, or personal computers, isn't it ludicrous to test typing speed and accuracy on electric typewriters? Not only is the touch different on various keyboards, skewing results, but what's most important is whether a candidate can use the equipment to its maximum effectiveness, not how fast he or she can type on it. The input, formatting, and editing of documents on high-tech equipment is a lot more complicated than straight typing on an IBM Selectric typewriter. Don't waste your time testing the typing speed of an applicant if what you really need to know is whether he or she can operate an electronic typewriter or word processor.

Many employers give a spelling test to applicants. I would recommend instead that candidates be tested on their ability to proofread and edit documents. You need a secretary who can pick up errors and correct them: someone who can spot a misspelling and look up the word, not a walking dictionary; someone to correct your grammar so you can focus on content, not form.

What about shorthand skills? The days of one-to-one dictating are on the way out, considered a prerogative of only top-level executives. It's a waste of valuable time for both manager and secretary to be drafting a document at the same time. It's proven to be more costly as well. A recent study by the Dartnell Institute of Business Research concluded that it costs $2.78 more per letter when a letter is dictated face-to-face than when it is machine dictated. While some type of speedwriting skill is valuable for taking down messages and instructions, formalized shorthand is not necessary for this.

The most efficient way to initiate a document is for a manager to create it directly on a computer terminal in his or her office. This is the practice only in certain companies, however. Managers elsewhere use dictating equipment or hand drafting.

Dictating equipment should be the method of choice in terms of high technology, although not all secretaries would agree in practice. It's most efficient in principle, assuming the boss is adept at organizing thoughts in this manner. Experience shows, however, that not all managers are skillful enough to use dictating equipment without causing serious frustration and distress to the secretary on the receiving end. Some give too few directions, others too many; many leave gaping blanks or erase a few words every time they turn off the microphone to collect their thoughts. Some even write out things first and then dictate the document onto the machine.

In any case, you need not ask whether a secretary has experience with dictating equipment. Anyone can plug it into his or her ears and type. Besides, no matter how much experience a secretary has with dictating equipment, it's rare for anything but the most simple cover letters to be typed right off the machine into final form. Either the manager makes revisions or the secretary needs to retype letters or other documents because what was typed doesn't look as good as it sounded or because of misjudgments in formatting. What you should ask, if you use the device, is whether the secretary will *tolerate* using it. It's generally not a favorite part of the secretary's job.

If you're not one of the lucky few with your own computer terminal and your dictating skills are not up to par, many secretaries consider writing things out acceptable, as prehistoric as it may seem. In fact, many secretaries prefer it. Sometimes, there is a problem with the manager whose handwriting resembles hieroglyphics, yet you'll be surprised how a good secretary will learn to read your scribbles and be proud of the accomplishment. Some actually enjoy the challenge—it's like solving a puzzle.

Other secretarial skills include filing and the use of the telephone. Filing, a term that underemphasizes the enormous task of records and information management, has become much more complicated since the days when everything was manually stored on paper in filing cabinets. Today's secretary must work within or even decide upon a combination of storage methods, including various types of microforms (reduced images on film) or disk computer systems. It's no longer just filing, it's data base management and the use of information-retrieval systems. You need to know whether a candidate has what it takes to follow whatever system your company uses or to set up what you need. The best way to find out a candidate's records management abilities is to ask for a description of past job experience.

As for the telephone, your concern should go well beyond a pleasant speaking voice. Telephone skills rely heavily on the use of an individual's judgment, tact, knowledge of business etiquette, and discretion. More specialized uses also may be important. Determine what you need in terms of the telephone. Is it sales or customer-service related or is it courtesy in the face of high-volume calls? Do you rely on your secretary to make calls on your behalf and, if so, what type of calls are they? The best way to evaluate whether a candidate has the telephone skills you need is to set up a typical example and role-play it with the applicant.

A candidate's technical abilities are the easiest secretarial skills to identify. But don't put undue emphasis on a candidate's technical skills—they're only part of the total picture. The other part of that picture is even more crucial to whether a secretary will be of value to you.

Discretionary Skills—The Intangible Essentials

Discretionary skills, largely gained through experience, are less tangible than technical skills yet are the heart of the seasoned professional's value to the manager. Discretionary skills are those that rely on judgment and each secretary's particular talents:

☐ *Interpersonal skills*—interacting and getting along well with others.

☐ *Communication skills*—getting the message across, both orally and in writing.

☐ *Decision-making skills*—considering alternative courses of action and selecting the best option for each situation.

☐ *Problem-solving skills*—identifying and analyzing problem situations and recommending solutions.

☐ *Information-handling skills*—deciding what to do with the massive amount of information that comes across a secretary's desk, involving collecting, organizing, prioritizing, and channeling information to the appropriate persons.

☐ *Public relations skills*—dealing with others, including outside contacts and clients, on the manager's behalf;

using diplomacy—representing the manager and organization to the outside world.

☐ *Perceptual skills*—serving as the manager's eyes and ears in picking up what's going on that he or she may be missing but needs to know and anticipating the manager's needs without being told.

☐ *Organizational skills*—creating order out of chaos and keeping the manager organized and on track at all times.

☐ *Overall good judgment*—handling situations in the boss's absence or without close supervision in accord with the boss's wishes, knowing what to say and what not to say, sensing whether to act or to check before taking action, knowing whether and when to interrupt or disturb the boss, knowing when to speak up and when to keep silent.

How discretionary skills apply to a secretary's day-to-day work will be discussed further in Chapter 3. For now it's important to realize that discretionary skills can be even more important to you than technical skills, even though they are harder to evaluate. You can judge a secretary's level of discretionary skills by how he or she presents past experience, both on a resume and verbally. But the best information on a candidate's discretionary ability may well come from references. This is where it's important to give more than a perfunctory check into an applicant's work history.

All Secretaries Are Not Alike

As discussed in Chapter 1, a common misconception is that except for differences in mechanical skills, one secretary is about the same as the next. Again, generalized use of the term *secretary* has resulted in a blurring of individuality among those in the profession. Each secretary has his or her own set of abilities, strengths, and special talents. Your particular circumstances will determine which secretary is right for you.

Career Versus Stepping-Stone Secretary

Let's start by talking about choosing between two basic secretarial types: the career secretary versus the stepping-stone secretary. The former has chosen the secretarial profession as a lifelong career, while the latter is using the profession to get somewhere else.

You probably think it's best to avoid stepping-stone secretaries because you expect they are likely to be unhappy and will make your life miserable. But a career secretary is just as likely to become dissatisfied. In either case, it depends on how well matched the secretary is to the manager and to the particular job.

Or you may think a stepping-stone secretary will be anxious to leave you for another job. It's understandable that you would like to find a secretary who will stay for the long run. But just because a secretary intends to make the profession a career doesn't mean he or she will be satisfied with the same job indefinitely. Unless you can continue to offer growth and challenge, the career secretary is just as likely to leave you as is the stepping-stone secretary.

In any event, it's not always a good idea to be overly focused on finding the long-term secretary. Building a relationship with a real professional that grows with both of you is one thing. But sometimes a team can stagnate as manager and secretary settle into the status quo. Some managers fall into the trap of finding it more comfortable to go on working with the same secretary for years, even though the relationship may be counterproductive.

Sometimes the secretary who is most willing to stay on year after year is precisely the type you most want to avoid—the unprofessional. This is the secretary who cares most about collecting a weekly paycheck, is depressed on Monday, can't wait until Friday, and basically cares little about the company, less about your work, and not at all about your career. Not only does the unprofessional not care about taking on new responsibilities, he or she resists any deviance from routine, which can cause you more daily frustration than changing secretaries every three or four years.

Rather than looking for a secretary who will stay forever, put your energy into finding one who is a good match for you.

Above all, remember you want someone who is career-oriented whether that career is secretarial or not.

Don't be afraid of the stepping-stone secretary. Offering what this kind of secretary is looking for will provide great incentive for high performance in the name of career advancement. Even if you know from the outset a secretary will only be with you for a year or two, at least you know that for that period you will be getting top-notch assistance.

Think about the job you have to offer. Does it provide opportunity for a secretary to learn about a particular field? If so, it may be just the place for the noncareer secretary.

Within the category of stepping-stone secretary are two basic types: the secretary shopping for an industry in which to build a career and the secretary who has chosen an industry and is hoping to get a foot in the door. The shopper wants to learn all there is to know about your field and is looking for a position that provides broad exposure to the essence of the industry. Be honest with yourself and the candidate. If you work in the corporate services division of an advertising agency, your secretary is not likely to learn much about advertising. But if you are an account executive, you have much to offer a secretary who wants to learn the ins and outs of the advertising business.

For the person looking to get a foot in the door, again, be honest. The first thing this candidate will ask is whether there is an opportunity for advancing out of secretarial work in your office. Never make promises, of course. A candidate must expect to earn any promotion. The applicant needs to know whether you have the power to help him or her reach aspirations and whether the position would provide the kind of exposure necessary to ultimately get ahead. If you do have control or can offer exposure, the foot-in-the-door secretary may be a terrific asset to you. He or she will be keenly interested in your work and have great incentive to do a terrific job. As the key to this secretary's ultimate success, you could benefit greatly for the time you work together.

If, however, an applicant seems to expect to get what he or she wants without earning it first, the candidate is being unreasonable and is not the secretary for you. General time constraints

Profile of the Ideal Secretary Checklist/Worksheet

About You

Work Style
  Morning/Afternoon/
    Evening Person
  Workaholic or Good-Time
    Charlie
  Work/Personal Balance
  How Organized
  Perfectionist
  Procrastinator
  Delegating Style
  Style Under Pressure
  Project Juggler
  "Operator" or "By-the-Book"
Personality
Strengths/Weaknesses
Quirks

About the Job

Industry
Size of Department
Physical Setting
Social Environment
Number of Managers to Be
  Assigned to Secretary
Support Services
Work Pace
  Fast/Slow
  Consistent
  Cyclical
  Unpredictable
Sales, Service, or Product
  Oriented
Goals
Overtime

About the Company

Size
Location
Configuration
Corporate Culture
  Progressive
  Conservative
  Creative
  Laid Back
  Staid
  High Pressure
  Growing
  High Risk
Values
Policies/Practices
Rules and Regulations
Unwritten Rules
Benefits

The Secretary You Seek

Career or Stepping-Stone
  (Shopper or
  Foot-in-the-Door)
Background
Level of Experience
Personality
Technical Skills
Discretionary Skills
Special Talents

Must Haves	Can't Stands
_____	_____
_____	_____
_____	_____
_____	_____
_____	_____
_____	_____
_____	_____
_____	_____
_____	_____
_____	_____

Profile of the Ideal:

_____

_____

_____

_____

can and should be agreed upon at the outset. It must be a two-way street as well. You will have much to offer the secretary in return for what the secretary is to do for you.

If you're on the fast track and are able to take a secretary along with you, then maybe the career secretary is the one for you. Within the career-secretary category, secretaries range from the most green—fresh out of school—to the seasoned professional. Your choice will, of course, be somewhat limited by the salary you can offer. If you're in lower management, chances are you cannot offer a salary the seasoned professional will expect, unless other benefits can make a lower salary palatable (see the section in Chapter 5 on a broad view of compensation).

How Much Experience Do You Really Need?

It seems everyone wants a secretary with "experience." But not every manager really needs a secretary with extensive experience. So long as a secretary has the requisite technical skills, it sometimes pays to hire someone right out of school with no work experience to speak of.

There are many pluses to working with an inexperienced secretary. A brand new secretary is fresh with enthusiasm and willing to learn. He or she is comfortable using high-tech equipment—that's what students learn on these days—and can probably teach you a few things in that department. New secretaries haven't had a chance to pick up bad habits or to be negatively influenced by the unprofessionals. They are more likely to look to a boss with respect rather than suspicion based on past experience. An inexperienced secretary can be molded and brought along more easily than a seasoned person who might have become somewhat set in his or her ways. If an applicant is intelligent and has solid technical skills, that may be all you need to turn an inexperienced green secretary into someone right for you.

The level of experience you will actually require depends on how much you need to rely on a secretary's discretionary skills. If you're well organized and don't need your secretary to keep you on top of what must be done, for example, it may pay to consider giving a very inexperienced secretary a chance. An inexperienced secretary often can work very well with a heavy work load in terms of producing documents, correspondence, and so on. Here a secretary has the chance to display enthusiasm and technical proficiency while learning all about your job, the company, and the industry.

But inexperienced secretaries may lack the necessary confidence or ability to act without guidance and cannot be expected to jump right in with independent thinking. They are more like sponges, learning on the job and seeking direction from you. If extensive outside contact or in-depth knowledge of your industry is required, a green secretary may be inappropriate if you're too busy to bring him or her up to a working level. But if there are others in the office who can help during the learning period, an inexperienced secretary can work out well for you.

Think hard about how much experience you need in a secretary. Managers commonly make the mistake of thinking, "I'm so busy and have so many deadlines, I need a top-notch, experienced secretary to help me meet my goals." But a very experienced secretary would be bored to tears in a high-production job, no matter how fast-paced. The experienced career secretary wants to utilize his or her expertise in those hard-earned discretionary skills, not waste away behind a word processor.

The seasoned professional works best in a situation that allows the exercise of his or her full range of talents, such as in an office where the manager is frequently out and needs someone to take over in his or her absence. The experienced secretary can keep operations running smoothly while providing you with peace of mind. If you depend on your secretary to keep your head above water when the sea is getting rougher and rougher, the seasoned pro is for you. A secretary with experience has a whole bag of tricks for protecting you from people you don't have time for and keeping you organized despite your best efforts to let chaos reign.

Bear in mind, however, that the seasoned professional usually likes to work with little or no supervision. To succeed with the pro, you must be secure enough not to feel threatened and be willing to stand back and let your secretary do things his or her own way. The pro knows his or her place and enjoys it.

There is room for all types of secretaries in an organization—career or stepping-stone, experienced or not. The question is which is right for you.

Putting It All Together

You should now have a good understanding of your needs and how a secretary can meet those needs. (Refer once again to the Profile of the Ideal Secretary Checklist/Worksheet on page 45 to be sure you haven't overlooked anything.) The final step is to prioritize your lists and come up with a composite of the ideal secretary to meet your needs.

Listing Your Must Haves and Can't Stands

Read through your lists and label what you must have. You should use this *must have* list so you won't waste time on applicants who don't fit the bill and you won't hire someone on impulse who may later turn out to be a nightmare.

Add onto your *must have* list those things about you that perhaps have caused problems in the past or that you think might present a problem in the future. Every manager has his or her quirks, and your secretary must be willing to put up with yours. For instance, if you expect a secretary to perform servile tasks, such as serving coffee, sharpening pencils, or running personal errands, it's best to state these things in the beginning. If you make your expectations known, a secretary can look at such tasks as part of the job. But if you treat such sensitive requests as though they were a requirement, you may come up against serious resistance later by someone who considers them unwelcome chores that interfere with regular duties.

Then think about those characteristics, habits, or idiosyncrasies you would put on a *can't stand* list. This is where you articulate what it is about a person that you cannot tolerate—your personal pet peeves. For example:

☐ Gum chewing/smoking/eating at desk.

☐ Giggling/gossiping/gawking.

☐ Moping/whining/silent treatment.

☐ Women in slacks/dangling earrings/no makeup.

□ Being interrupted/scolded/ignored.

□ Coffee breaks/long lunch hours/clock watching.

□ Indecisiveness/brashness/insincerity.

Your *must haves* and *can't stands* should, of course, be free of characteristics that are covered by equal employment opportunity laws.

Review all your lists and draw up a profile of the ideal secretary. Now you should have a clear idea of what you are looking for. You're ready to begin the search.

Where and How to Look for Your Secretary

Shopping Within Your Company

A good source of secretaries may be your own company. If a secretary is unhappy in a given position, it's better to keep that secretary within the company than have to fill two places from the outside instead of one. Cost estimates for replacing secretaries run from $7,500 to $10,000 when you include the selection process, training, and the learning curve. Hiring a secretary who already works for the company not only saves you the valuable time and effort involved in recruiting from the outside, but spares you the trouble of finding someone who fits your organization and reduces the learning curve considerably.

Some companies encourage secretaries to move around within the organization through job-posting systems. If you work for such a company, you may be lucky to find the mechanism already in place to help you. To make the most of a job-posting system, get as involved as possible in the posting process. Write your own position description rather than leaving that task to the personnel department and be as specific as you can. Don't be limited in what you say by a form that's given to you for this use.

Make sure word about your opening gets out through the grapevine as well as through the official process. The perfect candidate may not be actively looking for a new position and may not see your posting, but still may be interested in the right opportunity. Review applicant responses yourself—don't just rely on what you are told by personnel—and make your own inquiries about people who are interested in the job.

Even if your company does not have a posting system or otherwise openly encourage transferring from within, you can still shop for a secretary within your organization. Notice the secretaries with whom you come in contact. Don't necessarily look for a secretary who is so obviously unhappy that he or she is shouting it from the rooftops—dissatisfaction can be hidden under a smile. A secretary doesn't have to be unhappy to be interested in a new opportunity, either. Even a secretary who has been with a certain boss or department for a long time may be fair game. Anyone who is serious about career advancement will be open to hearing about an interesting opportunity, which, of course, you have to offer.

If you see someone you think might be right for you, it doesn't take much to find out whether that secretary would be interested in hearing about the position you have to offer. Discreet inquiries can be made through your network of trusted friends or other secretaries with whom you are familiar.

If you work in a company where secretaries don't change bosses as a matter of course, you'll have to think about the possible repercussions of your actions. Stealing a secretary from another manager sometimes can create awkward situations. You would have to weigh the political consequences of your actions. Ruffled feathers can be smoothed over most easily where the transfer could be considered a promotion for the secretary. If it's a lateral move, changing departments for variety serves as another allowable circumstance. Your only potential trouble can come if the secretary's current boss has real and dangerous power over your career. Some people take it very personally when they lose a secretary to another manager within the company, and an abandoned boss could become vengeful. You have to consider that possibility.

If you don't know of a secretary you would like to win away, it's still a good idea to tap into the organizational grapevine and get word out about the fantastic position you have to offer.

Someone you didn't think of may surface. Remember though, you need to sell yourself and the position on the grapevine so that word of your opening will be passed on in a good light (see Marketing the Job, p. 66). Here's where it becomes important for you to have the reputation of a good boss. It's commonly known that the only way for a secretary to get into Xerox headquarters from the outside is to take a job that absolutely no one on the inside wants. You wouldn't want that designation tied to your secretary's position.

If a search within the company fails, it's time to begin your outside search.

Dealing with the Personnel Department

If you are required to go through personnel to hire a secretary, you must still take an active role in the search and selection process. The personnel department is there to serve you; your personnel representative can serve you best when he or she clearly understands your needs. Nothing is more frustrating for a personnel representative than to send up candidate after candidate only to have them all rejected by a manager who can't give specific reasons for his or her disapproval. Your representative should certainly appreciate your help. After all, it's you he or she is trying to please.

To start with, become friendly with your personnel representative so he or she knows you personally, not just as a name on a requisition form. Be sure you clearly understand the recruiting method to be used. Will the position first be offered to employees within the company? If so, you will want to be involved, as previously discussed. Will an agency be used for outside recruiting? In this case, you might want to recommend an agency you know that has a good reputation. In fact, you also might let your personnel representative know about all the sources you've discovered. Ask if the position will be advertised. If so, send a draft of the ad you would like to appear (see page 53, Advertising Successfully).

The usual procedure is for the personnel department to do the initial screening of candidates and then for you to select from a group of semifinalists. Choosing your secretary is far too important to leave in the hands of a third party. Don't sit and wait for what someone else considers to be the two or three best candidates for your position. Get involved right from the start.

Make what you seek in a secretary as clear as possible. Use the profile you created in the previous section to give your personnel representative a specific description of your ideal secretary. Once you're sure you're understood, let the personnel department do what it does best: test for basic skill levels and screen for other organizational requirements. But don't be unduly influenced by test scores unless you understand the testing used. Ask to see the tests administered and decide for yourself whether they are meaningful in your situation.

With your guidance, a personnel representative can accomplish the tedious narrowing of the applicant field. Let him or her handle the paperwork; you do the interviewing. Only you can decide which candidate is right for you.

If your secretary will report to other managers besides you, you still should get involved in the selection process. In fact, the more influence you exert, the better. Everyone dreads looking for a secretary. And a principal manager who has the responsibility for hiring someone to please others in addition to himself or herself has an added burden. Share the insight you have gained in moving through this analysis process with the other managers, especially those with decision-making authority.

If you do not have the authority to choose the secretary, don't throw up your hands and leave the selection to fate. Put yourself in the active role. More than likely, the principal manager has not thought out the selection process as carefully as you have. He or she probably will welcome your help in outlining a selection process. You may be raising items he or she never thought of or didn't take the time to work through.

If you cannot control the selection process, look at your *must have* and *can't stand* lists and circle those characteristics that are most important to you. Then share your list with the principal manager and, if appropriate, the other managers to whom the secretary will report. If you work in the same area, on the same team, you may gain support that will be even more helpful in influencing the personnel department with decisions.

Advertising Successfully

Usually, many more advertisements for secretarial openings appear on any one day than one person can or will respond to. Therefore, it's up to you to write an ad that will catch a reader's eye despite all the other ads on the page. Your emphasis in the ad should be first to market the job and your company and second to make the candidate feel special before he or she even applies for the job.

Since many secretaries suffer from poor organizational treatment, it helps if your company can boast of a better-than-average environment for its support staff. Start the ad with something like, "Join a company that's terrific to its support staff...." Then you could specifically describe what makes your company good to work for: "We offer comprehensive benefits including dental, profit sharing, and bonuses," for example. It's a good idea to list any benefits you will offer, especially those reflecting a progressive outlook on the profession, such as: "Personal and professional growth are encouraged through tuition reimbursement and on-the-job training...."

Choice of Title.   Executive assistant, executive secretary, administrative assistant, administrative secretary, or just plain secretary are titles commonly used in advertisements. Probably the most desirable title from a professional secretary's point of view is executive assistant. However, this title really only implies a position of the highest level. "Executive secretary" is more a generic term, although it does still have some connotation of requiring greater-than-average experience. "Administrative assistant" is a term that was introduced because so many talented people looking for jobs don't want to be considered just a secretary. All the term does is focus on the administrative aspects of a secretary's job rather than the strictly secretarial. But since all secretaries carry out administrative functions to some degree, the term really is nothing more than a euphemism. Most applicants recognize that this title does not necessarily signify a more prestigious position. You can use whatever title you choose—in fact, just plain "secretary" is fine. What's most important is how you describe the position, not what you call it. Look at the publication you intend to use and see what heading is most commonly used. If more than one heading contains a substantial number of ads, read them closely to determine which category would better describe your position.

Discussion of Salary.   Applicants sift through ads based on the salaries they offer. You must, therefore, say something about salary or you will get no response. However, unless you are offering top dollar, don't mention a specific salary range. If you state a median salary, you will be lumping your position in with all the others in that same range rather than setting yourself apart. Be vague but seductive: "Salary commensurate with experience" is often used, but gives the feeling that the applicant will have to prove himself or herself. I recommend using "competitive salary." It's much more inviting.

Your Industry.   It's a good idea to mention your industry to spark the interest of a candidate. Don't, however, make the mistake of requiring overly specific experience in a specialty of your field. What you need is a person who will fit into the basic environment, and broad experience in your general field will satisfy that requirement. For example, a secretary who is familiar with banking certainly can learn what it takes to handle a job in loan documentation. Or a legal secretary with experience in real estate can quickly learn new terminology and procedures necessary for bankruptcy matters—what's critical is that the secretary be familiar with the legal environment. A secretary's skills are easily transferable— what's important is that the candidate have an interest in what you do and is motivated to learn. Don't overlook the fact that many secretaries are seeking a job change simply because they are bored with what their experience has encompassed. Once a secretary has mastered a certain field and has advanced as far as possible within that field, the challenge and stimulation of learning a new specialty may be just what is needed.

Describing the Job.   First and foremost, don't discuss the secretarial skills required in your ad. Stating "55 words per minute" makes a job sound unappealing. The applicant gets the impression that the job only involves typing. You can screen for skill levels later—first get the candidate's attention.

Choose one catchy phrase to set the mood: "challenging and rewarding role," "project-oriented position," or "unusual opportunity." Then focus on the interesting aspects of the job and be somewhat specific: "coordinating flow of activities," "planning and promotion of special events," or "managing day-to-day departmental operation." Overly general phrases, such as "diverse position," tell the reader nothing. If the position you offer is entry level, say "growth position."

Don't fail to mention any special features that set the job apart from the pack: advantageous location, near transportation or shopping, plush offices, discounts or perks offered to employees, and so on.

About the Ideal Candidate. Whatever you say should be a compliment in advance to the applicant. You indicate that you appreciate the difference between an average secretary and the true professional when you say: "Seeking polished professional" or "top-flight assistant needed." "Career-minded" or "career-oriented individual" has been used to death.

Reference to a "commendable work history" is far superior to asking for specific experience. Restrictions of an arbitrary three or five years' experience in a certain area may well keep a lesser-experienced yet highly motivated candidate from inquiring, so it's best not to get too specific.

Some other terms that are overdone are "bright" or "brite," "energetic," "self-starter," and "detail-oriented" (I'm not even sure what this means, but it sounds boring). Instead, use "ambitious," "motivated," "take-charge," "work-on-own type," "independent," "creative," or "intelligent." Use phrasing that shows some thought went into the ad, giving a more personalized touch: "We need someone with a special combination of intelligence, enthusiasm, and sense of humor to complete our fast-paced team."

Inviting Inquiry. If you are in an area where competition for candidates is extremely stiff, giving a phone number to call provides most immediacy. Candidates are more likely to pick up the phone to inquire than to write to an address or box number. If you've written a longer, detailed ad that really sells the position, consider using an address or box number. One school of thought is that really serious candidates will take the time to write. In any event, it's best from your point of view to screen initial inquiries by resume. Resumes are particularly helpful when hiring secretaries since you can tell a lot just by how the resume is organized, how professional it looks in general, and whether the candidate's spelling and grammar are up to par. If you decide to use a phone number, you still can invite those who pass the initial screening to send in a resume in order to be considered. If they're serious, they'll follow through.

Getting Help: Selecting an Agency

You may decide you need help with the recruitment process. You must be very careful about your choice of agency or your recruiting experience can be nothing but a frustrating waste of time. Here are some pointers for selecting an agency that truly will be a help rather than a hindrance.

Until recently, most agencies dealing in support staff were the placement variety. Such firms operate by collecting applicants and placing as many of them as possible. As job orders come in, the agency searches its files to find an applicant who might be right for the position. When an applicant walks in or responds to an advertisement, the agency goes through its job orders and tries to find a position suitable for that person.

New on the secretary-recruiting scene is the executive-secretary search firm. The services of this type of agency are directed more toward client needs. Executive-secretary search firms operate in the tradition of executive recruiting: Real searches are conducted through a network of contacts by following up on leads to find the right secretarial candidate for a client.

Recruiting agencies for secretaries are scarce at this time. It's a segment of the employment industry that is just developing to meet the increased demand for top-flight secretaries during times when there is a critical shortage of candidates. It's well worth your effort to seek out the true recruiting agency, since the typical placement agency experience can be a nightmare.

Ideally, agencies act as matchmakers between employers and applicants. You call an agency and place a job order, explaining in detail what you are looking for. You might assume the agency serves as a sort of career counselor to applicants, providing guidance in choosing the right job. The truth is that secretarial placement, especially in metropolitan areas, is really a cutthroat business—many agencies don't care about creating a match, just earning a commission.

One thing to remember: It's just as hard for agencies to find top-notch candidates as it is for you. And, since placing secretaries is its business, an agency must try to place whomever it has in order to pay the rent. Many use the shotgun approach: A representative will send you a list of applicants a mile long, but none of them will remotely resemble what you thought you ordered. After a while you start to think the person you seek isn't out there and you lower your standards. Finally, out of sheer exasperation, you hire the best of the lot even if you really don't feel the applicant is right for the job.

Here's how it goes from the applicant's point of view. Candidates are lured in by seductive advertisements about fantastic jobs with great salaries and benefits. The chances that the applicant will get to interview for those jobs are slim to none. If they did exist, they may have been filled by the time the applicant enters the office. Once the candidate is in the office, agencies listen to what a candidate thinks he or she wants and then, as if they didn't hear a word that was said, give the applicant a rundown on what jobs they have to offer. An agency uses every trick in the book—cajoling, persuading, making the applicant feel guilty—to get him or her to go on as many interviews as possible. Then, pressure is high for the candidate to accept the first job that's offered.

If secretaries were abundant, agencies would be competing with one another for corporate clients and would be more likely to provide the kind of personal attention you need. In light of the shortage, however, agencies compete more for applicants than job orders. Many an agency's goal is to get an applicant hired and keep that person hired until it collects the commission—about three months. After that it's not unusual for agencies to start calling the candidate to go on another set of interviews with promises of even higher pay and better benefits.

Here's an industry where computerization has in some ways served to worsen service to clients rather than improve it. By computerizing job orders, the so-called counselors within the agency can access all open positions known to the firm. Right off the bat, the agency representative who accesses the job order may be telling applicants about a client or industry they really know nothing about. Often the job data are sketchy because the software program allows only a certain amount of information to be entered about each job order. Or worse, the information may be completely inaccurate. A frequent complaint is that applicants take time off from work to go out on an interview only to find that the job has been filled or is not at all what he or she is looking for.

Of course, not all agencies fit this description. It does seem, however, that this type is the most visible and most accessible to both clients and applicants since it often relies heavily on advertising. You must take the time to find an agency that truly cares about serving you, the client. Your first clue about an agency is whether you are given any personal attention when you call to place an order. Notice whether you are asked for particulars about your company and the job you are offering or whether you get the feeling the representative is trying to finish with you as fast as possible. The representative should be willing to take the time for in-depth discussion about you, the position, your company, and the type of person you seek. A counselor who is interested in hearing numerous details presumably will pass along that information to applicants.

Check into the credentials of the counselor. There are those in the industry whose efforts not only serve you, the client, but also work toward enhancing the secretarial profession and the recruitment process. Seek those recruiters who not only have extensive recruiting experience but also bring to the job past direct experience as executive secretaries, which gives them a greater understanding of what it takes to create a successful secretary/manager match. The representative also should know something about your industry in general and the equipment to be used in your office in particular. This will help ensure that your agency experience will be a positive one.

All agencies conduct skill testing, but be sure you understand the scope of such tests and ask to see actual results. Don't rely on what you are told over the phone. Also, find out what their specialty is, if they have one. Some agencies deal primarily in certain industries; others handle specific position levels, either on the low or high end.

If you have doubts about an agency, a good check is to ask the applicants sent to you what their experience has been. More applicants than you can believe withstand horrendous treatment by agencies—basically because they don't understand how the recruitment process should work and are uninformed about their own choices in searching for a job. You can learn a great deal just by asking the people you interview. If he or she volunteers a choice horror story, your doubts about an agency may be confirmed.

Your best bet is to locate a professional secretary search firm. Recruiting firms that conduct professional executive-secretary search in the tradition of executive recruiting are few and far between but worth the effort of finding. Again, the key term here is *search* rather than *placement*. Professional executive-secretary search firms rely on referral networks for candidates rather than draw from advertising. Often, not every applicant who walks through the door is placed. In some cases, applicants must meet stringent requirements before even being considered a candidate by true recruiting firms.

The most elite of secretarial recruiting firms deal only in placing executive assistants with upper-level executives. With this type of serious search firm, involvement in the recruiting process goes well beyond the typical initial screening and skill testing of applicants. In working to find a real match between executive and secretary, these firms focus not only on basic job requirements, but on the psychological aspects of the executive and what kind of secretary best meets his or her needs. This type of firm, such as The Duncan Group in New York City, goes beyond usual reference checking by thoroughly investigating a candidate's reputation in the business world through a network of contacts. With top-level firms, the recruitment process is so comprehensive that the client executive finally is presented with two or three candidates, all of whom are considered not semifinalists, but equally perfect for the job. The client then only has to choose which one he or she likes best, rather than spend any time evaluating the candidates.

Of course, such personalized service is expensive. The ultimate in executive-secretary recruiting firms work on a retainer rather than a contingency basis. To give you an idea of fee ranges, the average agency charges 10 to 15 percent of the candidate's annual salary payable when the candidate has remained on the job three months. Executive search firms charge up to 30 percent of annual salary, with those operating on a retainer basis requiring half that amount in advance and the remainder becoming due if and when an applicant is hired.

If a retainer is more than you are willing to spend or if the secretary you seek is not at the highest executive level, you can still get proper treatment from a firm that operates on search principles but on a contingency basis. A quick screening process will turn up such recruiters, such as Julia Woogen of John Buckley Associates, Inc., in New York City. Ms. Woogen's tip for initial screening is to find out whether the agency sees applicants strictly on an appointment basis. If not, chances are the agency is not operating at the sophisticated level you seek.

Secretarial Schools

Other good sources of applicants are secretarial training grounds. Many corporate recruiters gain a competitive edge by approaching schools that train secretaries well in advance of graduation day. Secretaries are trained in many two-year state colleges and many private business, technical, and secretarial schools. Most, if not all, schools have a placement office where employers can place job orders and learn about potential candidates. Some placement offices charge a fee, although most do not.

Tapping the Secretarial Networks

See the Appendix for a list of secretarial associations, which often prove a valuable source of potential candidates.

Making the Right Choice

You're well armed with a profile of what you need in a secretary and with leads for where to find the perfect person to complete your work team. Now you need some tips on weeding through candidates, recognizing the right one for you, and convincing that person to accept the job you have to offer.

Prescreening a Candidate

We've talked at length about specifics. Now let's step back and look at how you'll know whether an applicant is in the running from your first contact.

The usual attributes one looks for in a job candidate are a positive attitude, reliability, initiative, honesty, diligence, and so on. When choosing a secretary, however, your first and foremost concern should be whether the secretary exhibits professionalism.

How do you identify an unprofessional? First, by appearance. The true professional knows enough to wear a business suit to an interview; the exceptional candidate will have researched appropriate attire for your particular office and will dress accordingly. Everyone should know the importance of looking his or her best when interviewing for a job. Therefore, don't give job applicants the benefit of the doubt when it comes to appearance. If that's the best they can do, imagine what they'll look like on a regular basis.

Next, pay attention to what the applicant says and how he or she says it. How does the applicant describe previous jobs? Does the candidate seem proud of what he or she has accomplished or only think of past performance in terms of previous bosses' jobs? Does the applicant seem enthused about the opportunities your job might offer or just interested in how much money it pays? Does the candidate have ideas for future career plans or is it evident his or her attitude is, "I think about one job at a time"?

Tone of voice conveys more than words themselves. Does the applicant's tone of voice convey confidence? Does the candidate sound calm and in control or nervous beyond what one might expect from an job applicant in general? You want someone who values his or her own ability to make a contribution. Look for someone who sounds able to do just that.

So much for evaluating surface clues. Your next consideration has to do with how a secretary can help you get ahead in your career. You need a secretary who understands the concerns of managers and management in general—someone who understands the importance of relating to company goals, not only self-interests.

The way to determine an applicant's perspective is to ask the simple question: "Tell me about the companies you have previously worked for." If the candidate can intelligently discuss the company's business, goals, and status in the marketplace, you're on the right track. If the applicant goes on at length about benefits, compensation, or vacations, you're in trouble.

Another important consideration is whether a secretary's locus of control lies within rather than outside of himself or herself. You can't benefit from secretaries who see past experience as a series of events that happened to them rather than situations they had a hand in controlling. Candidates who have long lists of reasons why past jobs were so unsatisfying and none of the reasons involves their own contribution are likely to see themselves as victims of circumstances rather than creators of reality.

Keep one exception in mind. Don't pass up what you think might be an unpolished gem. Try to tell the difference between a secretary whose established set of characteristics is undesirable and one who can be molded into the ideal. The unpolished gem might come across as eager to learn, although somewhat naive.

One final, crucial point is to be extremely concerned about an applicant's discretion. Never consider hiring a secretary who bad-mouths previous bosses. Take it as a clue that you'll never know what that person will say about you. Don't eliminate a candidate just because of a previous personality conflict with a manager, however. How an applicant chooses to relate the situation will reveal just how discreet you can expect that secretary to be.

Reading a Resume—Between the Lines

When it comes to screening secretaries, you can learn much more about a candidate from a resume than just past job experience. It is, in fact, a useful guide to a secretary's perspective and level of professionalism. Pay close attention to how a resume looks as well as its content. If a secretary's resume isn't highly appealing to the eye, it's a serious comment on what kind of secretary he or she is. It should be virtually perfect—set up attractively, with no typos or white-out, and carefully organized. It should reflect a true understanding of what duties were performed in previous jobs. If a resume lists only the usual secretarial duties, such as typing and filing, it's a clue that the candidate is unaware of how a secretary can function as a real team member and is oblivious to the importance of discretionary duties. If, on the other hand, a resume reflects insight into how a secretary contributed on the job, it's a good sign he or she will be able to do the same for you.

Notice whether descriptive paragraphs mention the business or industry of the employer. See if there is mention of the department in which the candidate worked. If the resume is nothing more than a chronological listing of past jobs but at least looks perfect, you may give the candidate an opportunity to provide an in-depth explanation of experience.

Prescreening by Telephone

The telephone has limited use in the interviewing process. It's an imperfect device for communication and is not an effective way to evaluate candidates. A person's voice tends to bring to mind a picture that rarely resembles the person on the other end, either from a positive or a negative point of view. Ideally, the telephone should be used only for the purpose of inviting candidates to forward a resume and cover letter.

If you are inundated by phone calls in response to an advertisement, you may want to use the telephone to determine whether an applicant will get to first base. To weed out unlikely candidates from the start, be systematic rather than subjective. Choose items from your *must have* or *can't stand* list to use as a guide. For instance, one management-consulting firm in New York City started out by asking every female applicant who called whether she had a problem with wearing stockings every day, even in the height of summer in the city. This is not the time to get into lengthy discussions of background or details about your position. You want to avoid prejudging an applicant in terms of past experience or skill levels. You could pass up someone special if you decide an applicant's experience is too light without even meeting him or her. If a caller's first questions have to do with money, you can feel confident ruling out that candidate, however. You want someone who is interested in a career-building job, not just bringing home a paycheck.

If you insist on prescreening by phone, a good method is to ask each caller a good open-ended question like, "What is your situation?" to get him or her talking. You won't learn anything if the candidate asks the questions and you do the talking. Decide in advance on the objective information you seek to learn as a result of the phone call. Again, when using the phone, don't rely on subjective reactions or you could be wasting your time or, worse, making false judgments.

The One-on-One Interview

You know what you want to find out. Let's talk about how you'll find out whether an applicant fits the bill. First of all, be prepared. Have your lists at hand and an agenda in mind. Don't wait until the applicant is sitting in front of you to review the resume. Read it in advance and take notes or, if you're reading many resumes and interviewing a lot of people, you won't remember what you meant to ask.

Avoid falling into the trap of applicants who say what they think you want to hear. You want a secretary who is as concerned as you are that the secretary/manager match be right.

I recommend, again, the use of open-ended questions that give you the opportunity to evaluate candidates based on how they handle their responses. You can uncover their level of self-confidence, how articulate they are, whether they have a positive or negative attitude, whether they talk too much or too little, and how discreet they are in addition to learning about whatever's on your lists.

Some ideas:

- "Tell me about your last job."
- "Tell me what you learned on your last job."
- "Tell me about your favorite boss."
- "Tell me what you're looking for in a job."

Don't ask what interests the applicant about your position, at least not until after he or she has had a chance to learn something about it. One purpose of the interview should be for the candidate to learn what the job has to offer. The candidate should show an interest in finding out what the job entails, rather than just attempting to convince you to hire him or her.

One good way to find out whether a secretary's working style is compatible with your own is to set up a hypothetical working situation and let the secretary tell you how he or she would handle it. The president of an advertising agency used this approach. He described a scenario in which the secretary would be required to make a decision in his absence that included whether to contact him. By the person's answer he was able to determine whether they were on the same wavelength.

Another good technique is to arrange in advance for someone to enter your office while you are interviewing the candidate. Introduce the guest to the applicant. How the candidate reacts will tell you a great deal about his or her level of confidence, ability to relate to others, sense of business etiquette, and in general, whether you are comfortable with that candidate's style.

Don't feel you must decide on a candidate after just one in-person interview. It's good enough for a first step to get a general sense about whether someone is in the running. You then can make notes and start the narrowing process on the next round. Invite the applicant to come back again in a few days, assuming, of course, that time allows it and that the person is not pressured to act on another offer. In the next day or so you may well think of things you wish you had said or asked.

Picking a Winner

By the time you get down to choosing between two or three candidates, you should have covered absolutely everything on your list. Don't get hung up on one issue to the neglect of others, and leave no stone unturned.

When it comes down to choosing between two or three semifinalists, chances are there will be pros and cons to each. That's when it's time to sleep on it and use your intuition. If logic tells you to pick one over another but something nags at you to choose the other candidate, follow that feeling. It is undoubtedly based on information you're carrying but are not openly aware of. The reason will reveal itself in time. If you ignore your inner voice, you may likely find yourself sorry later.

Marketing the Job

Now that you've zeroed in on the best candidate, you must convince that person to accept your offer.

Speak to the candidate as a colleague, indicating that you consider the secretary to be a part of your team. Tell the candidate about the job in as much detail as possible. The more a person knows about a situation in advance, the less anxiety he or she will feel about entering into it. If the secretary you want is deciding between your job and another one, chances are that candidate will go with what is the surer bet.

Convey overall that you are a progressive-minded boss who will treat the secretary as a significant part of the team. When describing the job, emphasize the nonsecretarial aspects of the position. Don't discuss the filing system or word-processing equipment. Tell the candidate what is accomplished by your company, your department, and about the types of projects you get involved in. Give examples of particularly rewarding situations you experience. Talk about the other people with whom the secretary will come in contact, emphasizing their good points. If your company will provide in-house training or pay for continuing education or seminars of any kind, let the candidate know.

Of course, you shouldn't promise a rose garden. Give the candidate as realistic an idea as possible of what it would be like to work with you. Be completely open and honest, including the negatives as well as the positives. Trying to hide the downside of the job will only create suspicion. Once you've made clear the overall scope, reveal special requirements of the job that might meet with resistance if left to chance, such as if you expect your secretary to do all of your copying, place all of your telephone calls, or serve coffee. Your overall message should be positive, yet realistic.

Encourage the secretary to give you and the company a try.

Making the Offer

Avoid the nightmare of finding the perfect candidate only to lose him or her to another job offer. When you make the offer, do it yourself; don't have personnel make the call. The personal touch means a lot. Make the offer in person, if you can. That way, you will have the opportunity to see the applicant's reaction to your offer and be able to clear the air about anything that is disagreeable to the candidate right on the spot. Small things that may not matter to you can lose you a candidate who is choosing between two jobs. Don't let anything slip through the cracks. Make it clear that negotiation in no way obligates the candidate to accept. You're just making sure you've done all you can to win over the candidate. If you've covered all bases and the candidate still chooses another job, at least you know there were no unanswered questions. Then you can continue your search without nagging doubts.

CHAPTER THREE

BUILDING AN EFFECTIVE SECRETARY/ MANAGER TEAM

What Do Secretaries Really Do?

Myth Versus Reality

If someone were to ask you what a secretary does, what would you answer? More than likely, your response would reflect the perception gap between what secretaries are believed to do and how they actually contribute on the job.

Most people, including many secretaries themselves, are hard pressed to describe what they do beyond the obvious—type, take dictation, file, and answer the telephone. The secretarial myth also includes stereotypical office wife duties—water the plants, serve coffee, order the boss's lunch, and shop for the spouse's birthday present. Ironically, although the term *secretary* is used so broadly that it encompasses almost any office worker who uses a typewriter, the stereotype still springs to mind when hearing the word. The truth is that there are as many different secretaries as there are secretarial positions and just as vast an array of duties and responsibilities that go along with them.

Do secretaries type, file, serve coffee, and run errands for bosses? Yes, most secretaries do some form of typing on word-processing equipment, a computer, or an ordinary typewriter. And, yes, many secretaries do serve coffee and perform other service-oriented tasks—and there's nothing wrong with that if it makes sense in a particular job. But this doesn't mean that's all secretaries do. To make the most of your secretary, you must move beyond the stereotype and recognize all that a secretary can do for you in a real value-added role. Let's take apart the job of secretary and see what really goes on.

A survey conducted by *Working Woman* magazine in September 1985 addressed the issue of what secretaries actually do. The survey listed many duties ranging from the most menial (serving coffee, sharpening pencils, ordering lunch) to what was termed "high-level tasks" (drafting letters, troubleshooting, doing research, editing and writing reports, preparing the budget, supervising others). The survey results reflected a significant gap between what responding secretaries said they are expected to do and what responding bosses say secretaries are expected to do (see chart on page 73).

Note that while there is a significant gap between what secretaries say they are expected to do and what managers say secretaries are expected to do, this gap is most notable when it comes to the performance of higher-level tasks. As *Working Woman* concluded, "the time for American managers to give their secretaries credit for the true nature of their work seems long overdue."[1]

As this survey suggests, there is much more to the secretarial job than typing and filing, or even drafting letters and preparing the budget. Let's get specific.

Technical and Discretionary Skills in Action

In Chapter 2 we discussed two basic types of secretarial skills. Now let's take a closer look at how technical and discretionary skills contribute on a day-to-day basis.

To recap, we're using the term *technical skills* to indicate those skills usually connected with secretaries, such as typing, filing, and answering the telephone. The use of good grammar, correct spelling, and familiarity with technical or industry-specific terminology also are technical skills of the secretary that benefit the manager yet often go unrecognized.

Discretionary skills are largely gained through experience, rely on judgment, and are hard to measure yet invaluable to a boss. Discretionary skills also encompass the particular talents a secretary brings to the job. Each secretary exhibits a unique blend of both types of skills in his or her daily work. Discretionary and technical skills are not separate and distinct from one another, but rather interact for the benefit of the manager. Here are some examples.

Typing.   Mastering sophisticated word-processing or computer equipment and software applications—the norm rather than the exception nowadays—is no simple task. It's one thing to simply type using sophisticated word processors or computers and quite another to take full advantage of what a system has to offer.

[1] "The Uneasy Alliance of the Boss and the Secretary," by Julia Kagan and Julianne Malveaux, *The Secretary,* May 1986, p. 106.

Two Different Worlds:
Do Bosses Really See What Secretaries Are Doing?

Secretaries and bosses report radically different versions of what a secretary is "expected" to do.

HIGH-LEVEL TASKS	Secretaries	Bosses
Draft letters	86%	57%
Troubleshoot	73	47
Do research	65	37
Edit/write reports	58	26
Supervise/train receptionist, etc.	41	33
Prepare the budget	23	10
THE "SERVILE SIX"		
Clean coffeepot	45	31
Sharpen pencils	45	32
Make personal arrangements for boss	39	17
Run personal errands for boss	38	17
Get boss's lunch	29	17
Balance boss's checkbook; pay his/her bills	13	5

Reprinted with permission from *Working Woman* magazine. Copyright © 1986 by Working Woman, Inc.

Word processors or word-processing software packages provide a myriad of functions that can be fully utilized only if the operator has the patience and interest to learn their capabilities and can think like a computer, so to speak. It's not a talent every person possesses. Whoever has the impression it doesn't take brains to be a secretary is way off base, particularly in this technical area.

And what of the pages that are typed? There's more to preparing an attractive presentation or proposal than just typing words on a page. Creative typing, as I call it, takes an artistic sense of sorts and a pride in making the extra effort to create a document that is a step above the rest. No matter the quality of a document's contents, the way it is presented has a significant impact on how it will be received by the reader.

Filing. Filing is an outdated term that once described putting pieces of paper in appropriately labeled folders for later retrieval. In the information age, filing has taken on a whole new meaning and added new value to the secretary's role. What once was called filing has now evolved into records management, information retrieval, or, in some cases, data base management. Even the most straightforward of records-management systems requires keen organizational and decision-making skills so that a manager can have instant access to whatever information he or she needs at any time. It's one thing to file a letter, quite another to create and maintain a system for tracking inquiries, storing resource materials, recording project expenditures, or maintaining a data base system. What we are really talking about here is another major discretionary skill of the secretary: information handling. The broader implications of this key discretionary skill will be further discussed later in this chapter and again in Chapter 7.

Telephone Skills.   Answering the telephone is a big area that requires varying degrees of discretionary skill. Letting you know who's on the line is basic, as is keeping a running log of what calls need to be returned in the course of a day. But what about the secretary who is able to remember which people are connected to each account and how important such people and accounts are to you at any given moment? Isn't this secretary even more valuable if he or she has a knack for picking up this information without it having been specifically provided?

Now consider the whole area of taking messages in your absence or when you're busy on another line. A secretary must know not just how to take down a caller's name and number, but what questions to ask and how much or how little of the message you need to know to follow through on the call. A secretary must not just answer the phone, but decide whether to interrupt you or how important it is to track you down to take the call or to deliver a message if you're not around.

One boss marvelled at his secretary's ability to seemingly pull names and numbers out of a hat. Sometimes Mark would have only spoken to someone once and then months later would want to get in touch with that person, at that point not even remembering his or her exact name. He'd say to his secretary, Clarice, "Do you remember that guy who called? He was a friend of so-and-so and he worked for some kind of clothing company. . . ." And Clarice would go to a file where she routinely kept names and numbers of people who weren't listed in the regular files and, more often than not, would come up with just who Mark was looking for. Mark often would say, "How do you *do* that?!" Now that's a secretary who's really on her toes.

Secretaries are known for establishing and maintaining relationships that exist purely over the phone with secretaries of other managers, colleagues, business associates, and others whose cooperation a manager needs to accomplish work goals. Considering the barrier the telephone can be to clear communication, a secretary must make full use of his or her communication and interpersonal skills to develop these relationships. This is no small feat. Secretaries proficient in telephone skills can be invaluable in dealing with vendors who may have hundreds of similar accounts. Their managers can come to expect prompt and immediate service just because of the relationship between the vendors and secretaries.

Discretionary telephone skills also include knowing what manner to use with different callers, thereby presenting an appropriate image on the boss's behalf when placing or receiving calls. Now we're getting into one of the most important discretionary skills of the secretary—public relations.

Public Relations. Secretaries act as liaisons between managers and all other people with whom they come into contact, both inside and outside of the company. Secretaries must be ambassadors, setting the mood of new relationships and creating first impressions of the company and you. You probably rely on your secretary's public relations skills every day without even realizing it. You're a busy manager dealing with many people who all want immediate attention. A secretary is your diplomat when you need a buffer between you and the rest of the world. A secretary is a client-relations representative every time he or she answers the phone or greets someone who comes to call. What would you do without the secretary who knows how to coddle that difficult client and hold him off until you are able to attend to him? And what would it cost if that client got fed up with waiting and didn't have that soothing voice to calm his nerves while he impatiently waited for you to speak to him? What about the customer who feels his call is crucial, even though you have five other crucial calls to return before you get to him?

Language/Communication/Interpersonal Skills. A command of basic grammar, spelling, and the English language is a technical skill, yet there is a discretionary side here as well. One secretary may be able to catch grammatical or spelling errors and correct them. Another, however, may be able to grasp your particular writing style and have a talent for drafting or editing your work to create documents indistinguishable from what you would have done yourself.

Communication skills in some ways are technical in that they involve clearly conveying a message both orally and in writing. But a secretary must not only relay information to and from a manager, he or she must also gain the cooperation of others to accomplish work goals. Communication skills, combined with interpersonal skills, take on a discretionary flavor when it comes to using diplomacy, being persuasive, or influencing others to act in a certain way on a boss's behalf.

Anticipating Needs. Secretaries make appointments and schedule meetings. It's one thing to fill an opening in your appointment book. It's quite another to decide how much time a person or a meeting will require or what times of the day to do certain activities and what times to keep clear. It's one thing to set up a meeting, call participants, and reserve a conference room. It's another to prepare the materials you will need for that meeting without having been told.

The Invisible Helping Hand

So far we've explored how typical secretarial skills really serve a manager. Secretaries also do many things to keep the office afloat that very often go unrecognized. Such duties often are automatically performed by a secretary, assigned little importance, and taken for granted even though they have a great effect on whether the manager gets his or her work done. No one stops to think about what goes into the job while everything is going smoothly. But when the secretary isn't there for any reason, things fall apart.

Let's talk for a moment about one disorganized manager, Susan. Papers tend to fly when Susan is around. Her desk and entire office look like a tornado struck. Yet, whenever Susan is looking for a certain file or document, her secretary, Marcia, always seems able to come up with it. What's happening is that while Susan never calls Marcia in and says, "Here are some papers that should be filed," Marcia takes it upon herself to go into Susan's office periodically to peruse the various piles of paper and organize them. She determines which documents and files relate to inactive matters (not needed for the last day or two) and puts them where they belong. Marcia laughs to herself whenever she hears another manager marvel at how organized Susan is despite how disorganized she appears. What's ironic is that Susan herself is unaware of just how the system works; she only knows that it does. This is just one example of discretionary organizational skills in action.

Many a manager is totally unaware of all the things a secretary does routinely that not only save the manager time, but also reflect well on him or her. This is especially true in service industries where clients are involved. As Diane, a legal secretary, relates, "Clients call and ask for copies of things or for non-work-related items, such as recommendations for a restaurant or hotel, for reservations to be made, or whether we know someone to contact here or there. There's often no need to tell my boss who called and what they asked for. I just do it."

Managers routinely send out packages that are extremely important or time dependent. Many assume that once a parcel is out of their hands, urgent documents will reach their destination because their secretary has chosen the best method of delivery. What they don't realize is that the secretary closely followed the package's progress, following up, checking, and double-checking to make sure the package not only arrived at the proper destination at the right time, but that it ended up in the hands of the right individual. The secretary's follow-through work often gets taken for granted.

In serving as liaison between the manager and others, a secretary often gets results without the manager even knowing how it was done. One boss, Fran, frequently needed information from the accounting department during the interval between usual reporting periods. Of course, it was up to Sharon, Fran's secretary, to get this information. Jerry in accounting was not easily approachable since he had more than enough to do just to keep up with his regular work, let alone manually compile information for Fran whenever she wasn't willing to wait for the monthly computer printout. Sharon worked hard to develop a relationship with Jerry so that he would cooperate with Fran's frequent requests. Sharon traded favors and offered to help in any way she could to smooth over Jerry's ruffled feathers. It was true that Jerry really had no choice but to comply, since Fran was his ultimate superior, but through Sharon's efforts, his cooperation was more readily forthcoming.

A Job's Particulars and a Secretary's Special Talents

Secretaries also use more specialized abilities depending on the office, such as financial management skills. They may routinely work on budgets, client billing, accounts payable or receivable, payroll, and the tracking of expense accounts; or they may get involved in negotiating, calculating, and controlling and reducing expenses. Secretaries often get actively involved in sales and marketing by promoting company products or services, actively selling, or answering inquiries. As more and more offices become updated and automated, secretaries are being called upon to research and select the equipment most appropriate for a company's needs.

How a secretary actually contributes in an organization largely depends on what the organization needs. Since the secretary's job is so often officially unstructured, secretaries many times just do whatever is necessary—filling the gap, so to speak. That requires the use of each secretary's special talents.

Carolyn was secretary to a vice-president, Anne, in a management consulting firm. This vice-president's job was to write proposals, create and sell training programs, and then conduct the actual training. Anne's forte was clearly in the selling phase of this cycle; her proposals were persuasive and her presentations were dynamite. But when it came to writing the actual training program, Anne was less enthused. Training just didn't hold the same challenge as selling.

Anne found, to her pleasure, that Carolyn was very interested in program development. Not only did she enjoy researching information to be included in programs, she really had a knack for putting together highly appealing training manuals. Since the training manual itself—to be kept by the client—was a major portion of the product, this talent turned out to be very important in ensuring a satisfied client. Anne and Carolyn were a team: Carolyn delivered to the client what Anne promised.

The benefits didn't stop there, either. Carolyn was so motivated by contributing to the team effort that her other duties were accomplished in record time. Anne seized upon every opportunity to capitalize on Carolyn's apparent creative talent, for instance, asking her to design an advertisement for the company's entry in a convention directory and including her in the creation of a new company promotional brochure. Not only was Carolyn motivated by such assignments, but the company won also by saving money.

You may ask at what point does someone like Carolyn ask for a promotion or more money? Certainly, at some point he or she will—and should. A person should be recognized and compensated for the value of his or her contribution. We'll cover that in Chapter 5.

Management Skills in Disguise

Many people think a secretary is a secretary is a secretary. Along with this line of thinking goes the belief that secretaries are not, nor could they ever be, managers. The truth is that many of the secretary's skills are in fact management skills utilized on a different level.

Planning is a basic management skill. Secretaries plan, too. A secretary must plan how to get work done on time by organizing a work load and determining priorities. Managers coordinate; secretaries also use coordination skills in accomplishing assignments by juggling time, people, and tasks despite constant interruptions by people and the telephone. They coordinate their work load according to the availability of equipment, working around peak times at the copier where sharing is required, for instance. Coordination also requires effective time management— well accepted as a valuable managerial skill.

Secretaries are not often thought of as decision makers. It's true that historically secretaries have not been empowered to make many decisions of bottom-line importance. But a secretary does make decisions every day, even though they are different from those of top executives. The decision-making process is the same regardless of what the decision is, however. A competent secretary needs a grasp of the process to be successful just as an executive does. Secretaries use decision making daily, especially in connection with information handling, prioritizing, organizing their work loads, screening telephone calls, and handling matters in the boss's absence.

Another of the secretary's key managerial skills is problem solving. Secretaries routinely use problem solving in connection with office administration and procedures, yet the skills involved in identifying and finding solutions for problems in this area are easily transferable to other work situations. And, as has been discussed, secretaries regularly exercise interpersonal and communication skills in their daily work.

So what *is* the secretary's role on the management team? That role should not be prejudged and cannot be generalized. Your secretary's function should fit your specific situation. Within your organization and department, your secretary should do whatever is necessary to best accomplish the secretary's purpose— that is, *to provide you with professional support in getting the job done.* Don't be boxed in by assumptions of what a secretary does. Continually look for ways to expand what your secretary can do for you.

By now you should realize that secretaries are not all alike and that few resemble the outdated stereotype. Look at your secretarial position and your secretary as unique. They are. Learn to make the most of your secretary's function and the special talents he or she brings to the job.

Making It Work

There's a saying that if you take care of the little things, the big things will take care of themselves. This philosophy can be adapted to the secretary/manager relationship. If the basics are in place, the environment will be ripe for development of a truly effective work team. Let's build a solid foundation and work our way up to loftier ideals.

In the ideal secretary/manager situation, the two work in sync with one another. Working as a team requires coordination of effort. You start by getting organized.

Getting Organized

Remember the old saying, "a place for everything and everything in its place"? You and your secretary should establish where to keep things you might need from each other. Set aside a special place for current files and working papers, whether it be a drawer of your credenza or just a corner of your desktop. Very often a secretary needs certain information while working on a document—perhaps the address of someone or the spelling of a name—that can be found in your working papers. It's more efficient for a secretary to find needed information on his or her own than to interrupt you or wait until you're available to ask you the question.

Also think of the things you might need from your secretary: general supplies such as folders, note pads, pens and pencils, petty cash slips, or other procedural forms. It's good to be able to help yourself rather than do without something because your secretary is out to lunch or is too busy working on a project to find something for you.

Your secretary needs to know where you keep your calendar and personal Rolodex file, if you have one. You need to know where your secretary keeps a Rolodex and how locally stored files are kept. You should also have a general idea of how to gain access to files that are not kept in your area, should you need something in your secretary's absence.

Set up mutually comfortable systems of operation. First, consider paper handling. Most people use in and out boxes for intercompany mail; use the same system between the two of you so you need not interrupt one another every time you want to move something to the other's desk. Decide whether to use a separate box for filing and agree on how often it should be checked. Using a "to be filed" box is helpful in keeping your desk clear, if you're one of those people who tends toward clutter. If you're just not the type to be diligent about a clean desk, think about having your secretary check your desk periodically when you're not around to look for noncurrent items that may be filed.

Set up a system for recording names, addresses, and phone numbers. If you maintain a Rolodex in your office, have your secretary routinely make up two cards each time a person is added. Let your secretary know of any special information you want included, such as a person's secretary's name, as well as how you like the information recorded—phone number at the top right and so on.

The Telephone

Set up a system for answering the telephone and placing your calls. Decide whether you will answer the phone yourself or have incoming calls screened. Keep in mind that continual interruptions to answer the phone or place a call are most disruptive to a secretary who is trying to get work accomplished. If you usually talk to almost everyone who calls after your secretary has announced who's on the line, you should consider answering the phone yourself. Even if you answer the phone as a matter of course, you still can ask your secretary to pick up all calls when you are in a meeting or need to concentrate fully on a given project.

Let your secretary know just how you would like the phone answered, including the combination of information to be relayed to callers: your name, the secretary's name, the department, a greeting, or question. Some examples:

□ "Ms. Jones's office, Sara Smith speaking."

□ "Audit, Sara Smith speaking."

□ "Good morning, Ms. Jones's office."

□ "Audit, Sara Smith speaking, how may I help you?"

If your phone is so busy that your secretary must pick up overflow calls, decide whether you want a log of incoming calls and how much information should be recorded, such as name, number, time of call, subject, or follow-up. A log will help you keep track of what calls you need to return in the course of a day or week.

Placing calls yourself is more efficient. If you do ask your secretary to place your calls, make it clear *in advance* what your secretary should say if the person you want to reach is not available: that the person should return the call, that you will call back later, or that you wish to leave a message. *Never* ask your secretary to place a call and then decide to squeeze in an errand. It's aggravating for a secretary to get someone on the line only to find out you've disappeared. It's generally not well received on the other end either.

Your secretary needs to know the names and relationships of people who are important to you and your work in order to make appropriate decisions when these people call: what to say, whether to interrupt you, what questions to ask, or where to route the call in your absence. Don't expect a secretary to instinctively know although, as has been discussed in this chapter, crackerjack secretaries often do. Make it a point to provide that information as a matter of course. Provide a list of significant people and update it periodically. Such a list is also helpful when your secretary is out for any reason and someone else fills in.

Choose a central location and device for keeping telephone messages in case your secretary is away from the desk when you are ready to return calls. Messages should be kept by your secretary until you are ready to handle them; if your secretary hands you a message every time a call comes in, you're bound to lose track of more than one. Here again a log can be helpful.

Setting Rules and Standards

Set out rules and expectations right from the start.

Hours of Work. Make your secretary clearly aware of what all the implications of 9 to 5 are to you. If you expect your secretary not just in at 9:00 A.M. but ready to roll at 9:00 sharp and not 9:06, say so from the start. If overtime without previous notice is the rule rather than the exception, your secretary must realize this from the start as well.

Be clear about lunch rules. Do you want your secretary to take a lunch hour at the same time you do or would you rather have him or her cover the phones in your absence? How much flexibility will you allow for the length of the lunch hour or when lunch is taken? Will your secretary be expected to occasionally or frequently work through lunch—without prior notice?

What are your feelings about conducting personal business at the office, whether during work hours or not? How do you feel about personal phone calls? What about time off for personal business during work hours?

It's a good idea to get all expectations out in the open. But bear in mind that flexibility is always well-received and, handled prudently and within company guidelines, can serve as a basis for trading favors when you need help above and beyond the call of duty.

Who Is Where? Rules should go both ways. Complaints are loud and frequent from both managers and secretaries that one often disappears without a word to the other. A good rule is that you will tell each other when you are leaving the work area. It's also helpful to include where you are going and when you expect to return. Even if you're just stepping away for a minute, it's important to let your secretary know, because a minute can easily turn into 15 if something or someone sidetracks you along the way. You should, of course, always let your secretary know where you are or how you can be reached so he or she can best handle callers in your absence. If you do not wish to reveal exactly where you are headed, you can at least provide a general direction so your secretary can track you down if need be. A secretary can be instructed to leave a message in an obvious place if called away from the desk for any reason, being sure to include the time and not just, "I'll be back in 10 minutes."

When you're out of the office at meetings or traveling, set up rules for calling in periodically. If your secretary will be absent on a given day, insist he or she call you as early as possible so that you may arrange for coverage.

What's Off Limits. We talked earlier about knowing where to look for things in each other's work areas. You also should set up rules about areas in each of your offices where the other is not to venture, perhaps a locked desk or file drawer. Also let your secretary know how you feel about others entering your office in your absence.

One secretary's experience illustrates how important this rule can be. Andrea's boss, Pat, was frequently out of the office and never said anything to Andrea about whether to allow staff members to go into her office in her absence. Andrea noticed Jacqueline, a manager of equal rank to Pat, entering Pat's office on two occasions when Pat was away. Since Pat had never instructed Andrea to keep people out of her office, Andrea was not sure how to handle this situation. On a third occasion, Jacqueline found Pat's office locked and asked Andrea for the key. Andrea refused to open the office. It was one thing to confront a superior about entering another superior's office, but it was quite something else to help that person through a locked door. Upon Pat's return, Andrea reported all three incidents to her boss. Andrea's instincts were right: Pat had noticed her desk had been rifled as a result of the first two incidents and so had locked her office this last time. From then on it was clear: no one except Andrea was to enter the office in Pat's absence.

Maybe you're not comfortable about even your secretary having access to your work space. If you want your desk and office left untouched in your absence, make that a rule as well.

Secretaries Aren't Mindreaders. As will be more fully discussed in Chapter 4, many secretaries complain they don't know what is expected of them on the job. Be explicit in your demands. If when you call in from the road you expect your secretary to be available and ready with a complete report, make that known so he or she can be prepared and won't choose to go out for lunch at the appointed time. If you want to be left completely alone for a certain time each day, say so. If you expect your secretary to make sure you leave on time for appointments, ask for help. Your secretary is there to assist you and can do so effectively only if you're clear about what you need. Don't leave things to chance.

Assigning Responsibility and Authority

Speaking of not leaving things to chance, clearly set out where responsibility lies to avoid mistakes and reduce anxiety. And remember, in those cases where responsibility lies with your secretary, always delegate appropriate and sufficient authority to enable him or her to carry out those duties effectively and efficiently.

Scheduling. Decide who is to keep your calendar, make your appointments, and where appointments are to be recorded. If you keep your own schedule on a calendar in your jacket, purse, or briefcase, set up a system to keep your secretary abreast of your plans as far in advance as possible. If you use more than one calendar, designate one as the official schedule to which you may both refer to avoid scheduling conflicts. Whether or not your secretary is responsible for scheduling appointments, *always* tell your secretary when you make an appointment for yourself. A secretary is asked many times in the course of a day whether you are expected to be in on this morning or that afternoon. It helps if he or she has the same information you do concerning your expected whereabouts at all times.

If you designate your secretary as responsible for keeping your calendar, also delegate and abide by his or her authority to make appointments for you. It's a waste of time to tell your secretary to set up a lunch meeting for you and then for the secretary to go back and forth between you and the other parties to find an acceptable date. Either give your secretary the authority to pick a time and date based on your calendar or do it yourself.

Travel.   The same goes for making travel arrangements. If your secretary is responsible for your travel plans, make clear your needs and wishes in advance and then give your secretary the authority to make choices for you. It's frustrating and a waste of valuable time for your secretary to run back to you with all the options available for your decision. Give enough information in advance so your secretary can make intelligent decisions on your behalf. In addition to the date of departure and return, here is what your secretary needs to know:

□ Your travel time preferences—the latest time you want to leave, the time you must arrive by.

□ Whether you are traveling alone.

□ Your desired class of service and seat preference—smoking or nonsmoking, aisle or window.

□ Your choice of airport (some cities have more than one)—whether you insist on nonstop or don't mind stopovers.

□ How you will pay—whether by check or credit card and your credit card number.

□ Whether tickets will be picked up or mailed.

□ Whether you will need a car—preferred size, special options, and so on.

□ Accommodations required—hotel preference and type of room.

□ Your desired method of transfer from arrival point to hotel or other destination.

□ The amount of travel advance you will require.

Ordering Supplies.   Your secretary should handle the ordering of supplies, including shopping around for the best materials at the best price. Here again, delegate the authority for your secretary to carry out this task; give your secretary parameters and allow the secretary to make the decisions. It's inefficient if an order cannot be placed until you have approved it, especially if you're too busy to do so for days or weeks. And it's aggravating go to the supply closet to find the cupboard bare because you weren't available to approve an order.

In Your Absence.   Many secretaries routinely hold the fort when the boss is away, yet complain their efforts are stymied because they don't have the authority to make practical decisions. Handled on a case-by-case basis, the wise delegation of authority in your absence can best keep the office running smoothly even when you're not there. Don't leave things to chance when you're away. Clearly set out what matters your secretary should handle, what matters can wait until your return, and what matters require your handling from afar. Give him or her express authority to follow through.

Establishing a Routine

The vast majority of secretaries and managers work together haphazardly—that is, managers assign work as it arises and their secretaries have no real direction, moving from one project to another as priorities shift. It's inefficient and even counterproductive for a manager to call a secretary in or go out to a secretary every time he or she thinks of something for the secretary to do. It's much more effective and better received by a secretary to work with a plan.

Regularly meet with your secretary to plan upcoming work activities and to monitor progress on ongoing projects. A routine meeting each morning to discuss what's to be done that day sets the stage for a productive day. Regular weekly meetings to outline the status of projects provides a solid basis for decisions your secretary must make about work priorities. These meetings should not be catch-as-catch-can; they should fill a regular slot on your calendar.

A secretary can only work on one project at a time and works best without constant interruptions—just as you do. Except in cases of high priority, curb the impulse to give your secretary new assignments as they occur to you and have your secretary refrain from running to you for a signature every time a letter is ready to be mailed out. Instead, meet with your secretary periodically to exchange what you need from one another, perhaps right before lunch or during the last hour of the day.

When You Share a Secretary

The reality is that most managers must share a secretary with one or more other managers or staff members. In this case it is even more important to develop a good relationship with the secretary, since you will in effect be competing with others for the secretary's help.

If it is your secretary's designated responsibility to keep a senior manager happy above all others, you first must make sure your relationship with the secretary is such that he or she will at least do as much for you as humanly possible. If the secretary's best is still not enough, you may have to rely on the good will of other secretaries in the office to fill the gap. The keys to success in this case are maximum consideration and large doses of appreciation for help received.

In most other situations, the secretary should complete work in terms of priority. Number one, be honest about the priority of your work. You won't win any points with a secretary if you're always pushing for your work to get completed first regardless of its urgency. When conflicts arise over whose work is more urgent, don't put your secretary in the middle; confront the involved manager directly and settle the matter between the two of you.

When asking a secretary for what amounts to a favor, whether you're asking your own secretary to put your work ahead of someone else's or you're asking another secretary to help you out, *never* make your request a demand. Always remember the old saying about catching more flies with honey. Overbearance will certainly move your work to the bottom of the pile if it gets added to the pile at all.

Some secretaries tend to complete work for the highest-ranking boss first, regardless of priority, or for the manager with whom the secretary shares the best relationship. If you're the lucky manager, you may be tempted to leave it at that. However, in fairness to all, remember how it feels to be on the short end of the stick and encourage your secretary to consider everyone's needs and not just your own. The best way around this situation is to develop a system for keeping track of the secretary's work assignments. A log can be used to record work assignments, assigning managers, the estimated time needed for completion, and due date. The log keeps the secretary from showing favoritism, lets him or her stay neutral in case of conflict, and provides a basis for settling disputes.

Regular meetings should be held between the secretary and managers as a work unit. At such meetings, the managers can share their anticipated work needs for the coming week, two weeks, or whatever, and the group can work out a tentative plan for meeting everyone's needs. It also helps to have the secretary attend regular staff meetings to gain a clear understanding of how each individual's projects fit into the total department picture. You also should meet on a one-on-one basis with your secretary to keep the relationship on an even keel, to clear up problem situations before they grow out of control, and to find creative ways for your secretary to contribute to the accomplishment of your work goals.

If you experience periods where your work isn't getting done because the secretary is overly burdened, look into the possibility of hiring a temporary secretary to help with the overflow. If your secretary is seriously overextended on a regular basis, it's time to prove the need for more help. A well-documented appeal may convince upper management to hire another secretary, perhaps at least on a part-time basis.

If it's accepted that the secretary is indeed overburdened, yet no relief can be granted because of budgetary or other considerations, make an extra effort to ease the stress created by the secretary's work load. Simple acts of consideration will go a long way. Offer to do your own copying and collating when possible, for instance. Invite your secretary to lunch or offer to bring a soda or cup of coffee to break up the day. Above all, take a few minutes out of your own busy schedule to talk to your secretary about how the work is going. Sometimes just having someone to listen about how difficult it is to keep up with the work is all a secretary needs to catch a second wind.

Getting the Most From the Secretary/Manager Relationship

To take best advantage of the secretary/manager relationship, you must recognize and utilize the full range of your secretary's talents. A good place to start is with information—the focus of the secretary's role.

Your Information Manager

Here are some of the things a secretary can do with information:

☐ Analyze it.

☐ Compile, control, convey, condense it.

☐ Distribute, deliver, evaluate, expand it.

☐ Obtain, organize, process, present it.

☐ Research, review, record, retrieve it.

☐ Study, summarize, supply, store it.

☐ Translate it.

Take advantage of the secretary's vantage point and involve your secretary in the information-processing aspects of your work to save time and improve efficiency.

Do not have your secretary just open the mail but prepare it to provide you with instant access to what you need to know. Your secretary can peruse, sift, sort and prioritize, screen, summarize, and comment on incoming mail. If you routinely receive mounds of unsolicited mail, explain how you would like material handled—what pieces should be discarded, where others should be routed, and so on.

Common requests or inquiries requiring routine responses can be handled completely by your secretary with proper instruction. If you receive lengthy journals, reports, or other memoranda, have your secretary read and summarize them, highlight pertinent sections, and perhaps prepare an abstract for you.

In short, don't limit your secretary's participation to mere paper stacking. Allow your secretary to get involved and exercise intelligence in actually helping you process the enormous amounts of information you must deal with in your work.

Information handling should not be limited to what is on paper either. Information travels by telephone and through the people with whom you and your secretary, on your behalf, come in contact. Do not have your secretary just answer the phone or relay messages between you and others, but keep records of contacts, relationships, and the progress of projects.

Your Eyes and Ears

So much for the practical aspects of information handling. In the role of communications link between you and others, your secretary can effectively function as your eyes and ears. You can't be in all places at all times; indeed, you are often busy behind closed doors or on the road conducting business. If you do not benefit from your secretary's perceptual skills, you exist in isolation.

Secretaries are privy to a realm of information above and beyond the official meetings and memos that otherwise keep you informed. Even if you're on the grapevine, your secretary has access to a different perspective of what's going on in an organization. A secretary who is a link in the informal communication chain of a company has a finger on the pulse of that organization. You can find out, for example, how others reacted to your ideas at a meeting, who's gunning for your job, who's looking for another job, who's maligning you, or who's admiring you. If you're not tapping into this powerful information source, you're losing out on invaluable help.

One manager, Henry, routinely relied on his secretary's exercise of what he dubbed "prudent power." Henry used this term to describe how his secretary, Devan, influenced his actions by sharing with Henry her thoughts and ideas about goings-on in the office, as well as by providing him with information he might not otherwise come by. He called this influence prudent because Devan was always careful not to be overly pushy in expressing her opinions and, according to Devan, always was careful to express her respect for Henry's authority.

Henry found that Devan's access to information and personal insights often provided him with the missing pieces he needed to solve many everyday work puzzles. In one case, Henry had to replace a key manager in his department. Very particular about new employees, Henry spent six months choosing the new manager. It was clear soon afterward that the manager was not going to work out. As Henry discussed the situation with Devan, she shared her idea that someone already on the staff was a strong candidate for the position. Devan's suggestion was based on her solid knowledge of what Henry sought in a manager, having worked with him for several years, and on seeing in this staff member just the qualities she thought would fit Henry's requirements. Although the matter was never discussed again, the staff member in question was promoted to the manager slot. While Devan doesn't feel entirely responsible for the promotion, she does believe her contribution had some impact on how Henry saw the situation.

In another instance, Devan's grapevine connections provided Henry with information that saved the department from a potentially serious problem. Devan heard that the company's credit union was planning to move into the space directly adjacent to Henry's department, internal audit. Since the effectiveness of internal audit requires that the department remain detached from other company departments, confidentiality of its operations is crucial. This confidentiality certainly could be compromised if a credit union were operating right next door, with people coming and going by the department all day. With Devan's advance warning, Henry was able to stop the planned move before it took place.

Henry called Devan his "SRA"—strong right arm. That's what your secretary can be for you.

Your Strong Right Arm

We've talked specifically about how a secretary can help you manage information. Now let's take a broader look at the issue of delegating to your secretary. It has been estimated that executives spend an average of 53 percent of their time performing tasks that could be handled by secretaries. Examine your work habits and determine where delegation is in order.

Diane, a legal secretary, tells how attorneys often waste valuable time on client billing by relying on their secretaries merely to do the typing involved. Diane's boss, on the other hand, has her handle complete billing preparation, from gathering and double-checking fee and expense figures, preparing activity descriptions, and putting everything into proper billing format to writing cover letters. Ed has only to review the bills, if he desires, and sign the letters. Of course, Diane did not take on the entire task overnight; first she had to prove her ability by drafting bills for Ed's approval. When it became clear she didn't need Ed's input, Diane was given full responsibility, including handling any follow-up inquiries clients might have.

Tasks that can be delegated fall into three main categories—project work, administrative project work, and office administration. Here are a few sample activities under each category to start you thinking about how your secretary can do more for you:

PROJECT WORK

☐ Draft/edit documents
   letters, proposals, reports, etc.

☐ Conduct research
   obtain/retrieve information
   read/summarize data

☐ Communicate with clients, superiors, subordinates
   explain, instruct, respond to, consult with, interview, counsel

ADMINISTRATIVE PROJECT WORK

- ☐ Arrange, prepare for, attend, and take notes at meetings
- ☐ Create/revise/update meeting or project materials
- ☐ Schedule appointments
- ☐ Coordinate travel arrangements
- ☐ Train and supervise others
- ☐ Make collection or sales calls

OFFICE ADMINISTRATION

- ☐ Order supplies
- ☐ Maintain inventory
- ☐ Design and improve office procedures
- ☐ Organize recordkeeping
- ☐ Handle finances
   prepare budget
   track expenses
   prepare, follow up on billings

MISCELLANEOUS

- ☐ Answer inquiries
- ☐ Handle complaints
- ☐ Troubleshoot
- ☐ Improvise

Far from complete, this list doesn't even touch on how a secretary can creatively contribute to the particular work done in your department. A secretary's abilities and special talents will unfold as you provide opportunities for them to be displayed and developed.

As secretary to the director of corporate communications of a large corporation, Kathy was as surprised as her boss, Tim, to discover skills she possessed that, as she put it, "I didn't realize were things everyone couldn't do." Tim handled speech writing for top company executives. As Kathy typed the speeches, she found it made sense to arrange copy according to phrasing rhythm and natural breaking points. Picking up on Kathy's apparent talent after the first couple of instances, Tim gave her free reign in speech setup, leaving Tim to concentrate on the words themselves. Kathy's efforts proved extremely helpful to speakers, and the quality of the finished product reflected well on both Kathy and Tim.

Kathy's talents appeared in other areas as well. Public affairs regularly put out a daily news briefing that consisted of news clippings of interest to company employees. In her work with electronic data bases, Kathy found a way to access a synopsis of daily news highlights on international, economic, and domestic levels. She then figured out how to transfer the summary from the data base into her word-processing system, where she formatted it to be combined with the other news clips. Kathy's talents in moving in and around the data bases and computer equipment greatly increased the value of the daily news briefing. She was in effect publishing a daily newspaper for employees.

Be secure enough to delegate to your secretary. Anything he or she can do to help make more valuable use of your time only makes you look good in the long run. Find areas in which your secretary can help by inviting suggestions on your project work.

Joyce was executive secretary to the vice-president of economic research in a large corporation. Steven's work involved extensive use of visual aids—graphs and charts on 30-by-40-inch poster board and flip charts—for both in-house meetings and client presentations. Steven would show work in progress to Joyce and ask for her thoughts and suggestions for improvements. Finding Joyce's input valuable, Steven began to ask her help in the actual preparation of graphics, a little at a time. As it became clear Joyce could handle entire projects on her own, Steven just made the assignment and left Joyce to her own design, so to speak. Joyce went on to take courses in graphics, and when Steven retired and was replaced by a woman with no artistic talent whatsoever, Joyce took over full graphics responsibility for the department.

You have nothing to lose and everything to gain by delegating to your secretary. The result will be increased productivity and efficiency and a motivated employee—and nothing makes a manager look better than motivated subordinates.

Fostering Growth and Encouraging Creativity

Be open to suggestions on your work. Expressing an interest in your secretary's suggestions will stimulate more ideas and inspire your secretary to find more ways to help you. If an idea is good, say so; if a suggestion won't work, use tact in explaining why so your secretary can benefit from your knowledge and experience.

As you uncover potential, help your secretary's development by encouraging and, if possible, offering appropriate training. Look into training available within the company that could benefit your secretary or gather information on outside training programs to pass along to your secretary. Training not only promotes professional growth, but is a proven motivator and, as will be discussed in Chapter 5, can be used as a valuable perk for your secretary. A side benefit for you, as catalyst, is the pride you will experience as you see your secretary grow.

Building Trust and Cultivating Loyalty

A Secretary Is Loyal to a Boss Who Is Admired and Who, in Turn, Respects the Secretary.   High on the list of admirable qualities in a boss are honesty, integrity, intelligence, diligence, and loyalty to subordinates. Secretaries agree that respect must be earned, not demanded. A secretary respects a boss who treats others, including the secretary, as equal human beings. As one secretary puts it, nothing kills loyalty like a "peel-me-a-grape" attitude.

A Secretary is Loyal to the Boss Who Exhibits Trust.   Dare to confide. A secretary takes pride in what that title means—keeper of secrets. Start by conveying your belief in the importance of confidentiality and share tidbits of information. As your secretary proves worthy, take him or her further into your confidence.

Allow your secretary to exercise judgment and prove he or she is capable of handling work assignments, managing time, and meeting deadlines without your intervention. Curb the impulse to get involved in every situation—give your secretary room to handle responsibilities without overly close guidance or assistance. Give the benefit of the doubt. If your secretary doesn't appear as busy as you would expect or seems to be on the phone too much, don't jump to conclusions. Everyone has his or her own way of completing work assignments. What should matter is results.

A Secretary Is Loyal to a Boss Who Is Trusted. A secretary learns to trust a boss whose behavior is consistent with his or her words—in the smallest matters and in those of great significance. A secretary learns to trust a boss who stands behind his employees, who doesn't use people as scapegoats, and who backs up staff members when the need arises.

A Secretary Is Loyal to a Boss Who Shows Consideration for a Secretary's Needs. If your secretary attends evening classes, don't ask him or her to work overtime on school nights. If the secretary needs to catch a certain bus or train, take care not to cause him or her to miss it. Gail's experience is instructive. Tim understood that Gail required advance notice to make child-care arrangements in order to work overtime. Once arrangements were made, she could stay as late as necessary and often did work until 9, 10, or 11 P.M. — until the job was done.

CHAPTER FOUR

TALKING WITH YOUR SECRETARY

Communication: The Key to the Secretary/Manager Relationship

Consider the following statistics from a survey of 4,000 secretaries conducted in 1986 by Panasonic Industrial Company and Professional Secretaries International:

☐ Seventy percent experienced a lack of communication with their supervisor.

☐ Nearly half felt inadequately informed on their firm's overall objectives and the goals of their own work.

☐ Thirty-eight percent complained they don't know what's expected of them on the job.

☐ Fifty-three percent felt there should be better communication concerning work priorities.

These results certainly point to communication as a critical issue in the effectiveness and success of the secretary/manager relationship. The study, which focused on the causes of secretarial stress, revealed that lack of communication was the fourth most stressful characteristic of the secretary's job. You can be sure that this does not translate into productive and happy working situations.

Faulty communication between a manager and secretary hurts their relationship two ways: First, a secretary who is not fully and accurately informed can't work at maximum levels. A secretary's major role is that of information processor. How can a secretary successfully fulfill this role if a manager doesn't provide the necessary information? Second, less-than-satisfactory communication patterns can be demoralizing to a secretary. Not only is it extremely frustrating for a secretary to work without required information, it can feed a sense of unimportance, which then leads to discontent.

As a manager, you must be concerned not only with providing your secretary with everything he or she needs to know to accomplish work goals, but also with your own overall communication style. Without consciously working at this crucial area of the secretary/manager relationship, all other attempts at building and maintaining a productive, successful relationship will be wasted. Communicating effectively with your secretary is not a difficult matter—but it does require more than remembering to say, "thank you."

Manager-to-secretary communication has many problem areas, and most manager/secretary teams experience difficulty in many, if not all of them. Most complaints, however, are variations on a theme: The manager tends to overlook the secretary, failing to share enough information for the secretary to work most effectively. Many secretaries also complain that whatever information is conveyed comes cherry-coated, as if managers don't expect secretaries to understand.

Again, apply your perspective as a contemporary boss. Your overall communication style must show your regard for your secretary as a professional and as a member of your team. Here are some specific guidelines for a successful communication relationship with your secretary.

Guidelines for Effective Manager/ Secretary Communication

Conveying Organizational and Departmental Goals

It's startling how many secretaries are totally in the dark about the goals and objectives of the companies they work for— nearly 50 percent of those responding to the survey we just cited. Whether it's merely an oversight or because someone in the upper ranks doesn't think secretaries need to know, the result is the same: Secretaries feel unconnected to the work they do. It's no wonder so many secretaries feel isolated. No one bothers to tell them just what it is they're supposed to be accomplishing by showing up at work every day.

Think about how many meetings you've attended to be reminded of your company or department goals. It's probably more than you'd care to count. If your company has forgotten to fill in your secretary on the overall objectives of the organization, step in and fill that gap. Then make sure your secretary is fully aware of your department and your specific work goals as well. Communicate to your secretary not just the content of goals, but also the importance of what it is you're doing so that he or she can feel pride in participating. Invite your secretary to meetings whenever possible. Don't assume what goes on is nothing your secretary needs to know.

The purpose of clarifying goals goes beyond lofty ideals of engendering a sense of connection and building a team spirit. Knowing the overall strategy helps a secretary to effectively prioritize and allocate time to given projects. An uninformed secretary can be a roadblock to success by spending too much precious time on one activity to the neglect of other, more important ones.

As a team member, your secretary must not only know what the team is doing, but also his or her part in accomplishing goals. Make your secretary aware of how he or she fits into achieving team goals. Let your secretary know precisely what is expected of him or her. An informed secretary is your best ally.

Keeping Your Secretary Up To Date

If your work pace resembles white rapids more than a babbling brook, keep your secretary current on up-to-the-minute changes in priority or he or she will drown in the undertow. Fill in your secretary and briefly explain why a situation has changed. Nothing is more aggravating for a secretary than to be working on a super rush job all day, knowing nothing about it other than it must go out today, only to find at 4:00 P.M. that it's no longer needed. The secretary feels like the manager is capriciously pulling strings. After repeated episodes, the secretary will view the manager as the boy who cried wolf, will conclude that nothing is really a super rush job, and won't respond to emergencies.

A smart manager explains how his or her supervisor had asked for the super rush in a frenzy in the morning and then received an emergency call in the afternoon on a different matter that superceded the original rush. Now the secretary can commiserate with the boss about the lousy day they're both having rather than react as though he or she is the cause of it.

In addition to changes in priority, keep your secretary informed on the progress of projects. Fill in your secretary on what's happening, especially the more interesting aspects of a project. When you go to a meeting, for example, don't just tell your secretary you're going to such and such a place at such and such a time. Explain why you're going and the purpose of the meeting. Don't assume your secretary isn't interested or, worse, wouldn't understand. You'd be surprised how much many secretaries pick up just from typing documents.

Knowing more about a project than what is seen on papers that cross his or her desk makes the work more meaningful, creates interest, and motivates your secretary to do an even better job in participating in that project, whatever that participation may entail. Further, a secretary who is kept abreast of the status of projects is better able to anticipate a manager's needs. Knowing that you're tense because you're waiting for a call on a given project can help your secretary decide on a course of action during that day, for example. If your secretary is unaware of what you're experiencing, he or she may inadvertently add to your anxiety by bothering you with matters that are better left until later.

This is not to suggest that you spend hours on end sitting around gabbing with your secretary. It only takes a couple of seconds to pass along bits of information and will go a long way to further drawing in your secretary as a real part of the team.

Don't forget your secretary at the conclusion of a project, either. Secretaries often complain about working long hours on a project and then not being directly informed of its outcome. Many a manager has made the mistake of receiving the call that a client accepted a proposal, for example, and running straight past the secretary's desk to share the good news with other managers. Your secretary works just as hard as you do, although in different ways, to accomplish your work goals. Share the good news as well as the bad with your secretary. It will go a long way in building a successful relationship.

Giving Clear Directions

First, make sure your secretary is aware of all aspects of a project. You'll get much better results on individual assignments if your secretary understands the larger picture. Remember to pass on the background of the project, the names and relationships of all those involved, and other relevant information in case a question arises when you're not around. It's humiliating for a secretary to get an urgent call on a matter and not to have a clue as to how the caller can be assisted in your absence. A secretary put into such a position feels stupid and embarrassed—not to mention furious with the manager who created the situation.

Remember that descriptive terms such as *soon, quickly, right away,* and so on mean different things to different people. *Later* to you might mean this afternoon; *later* to your secretary may well mean tomorrow. Be specific. If you mean this afternoon, say just that. Further, don't throw papers at your secretary as you are running down the hall. This kind of behavior causes secretaries to throw up their hands before they begin.

There's a plaque some secretaries keep on their desks that laments, "There's never enough time to do it right, but there's always enough time to do it over." It only takes a few minutes to explain carefully exactly what you need and when. Time spent at the outset always saves time and aggravation later.

Don't try to do three things at once when giving directions. If you're explaining an assignment to your secretary at the same time that you're dialing the phone and looking for something on your desk, chances are your directions will be less than complete. Further, you'll miss your secretary's reaction to what you're explaining. Take the time to notice whether your secretary seems to understand your directions. Even if your secretary has questions, it's unlikely those questions will be asked if you appear too busy to take the time to answer. Time will be wasted, errors will likely be made, and your secretary will be frustrated to boot.

Giving Productive Feedback

Your secretary needs feedback on performance, both positive and negative. If there's something your secretary does particularly well, take the time to say so. If there's something he or she does that does not meet with your expectations or needs, you must share this too—no matter how small a detail it might seem.

Take Al, for instance. Al was very satisfied with his secretary, Jan, overall. In particular, she was great on the phone with clients. She remembered their names, recognized their voices, and knew what to say and what not to say to each about the status of his or her accounts. The only problem was that Jan routinely didn't pick up the phone until the third or fourth ring. Al felt anxious every time the phone rang that the client was kept waiting too long. It became an obsession. What to say to Jan?

As in all cases of giving feedback, when the message is negative, be sure to point out the positives as well so that the recipient of the information doesn't feel like a total failure. Al pointed out to Jan all of the ways in which she is terrific on the phone and how much he appreciated her talents in this area.

Al then said, "There's just one thing. Please make it a point to pick up the phone on the first ring if at all possible. It's helpful and I believe considerate to save even a few moments of the client's time. But most important, a ringing phone is one of those things that just gets to me."

Jan could argue that there's really no difference to a caller between hearing one ring or three. But because Al presented the situation as a pet peeve of his, Jan can neither argue nor take offense. Everyone is entitled to their idiosyncrasies — especially the boss.

Giving regular feedback is extremely important to the success of your relationship and to motivating your secretary. Remarks concerning performance should not be saved until an official yearly review. For feedback to be effective it must be provided close to the behavior exhibited. In other words, if your secretary did a great job putting together your materials for an important meeting, don't wait until the next time you're assigning something to say, "You did such a great job on my last set of meeting notes, here's another set. I need it in ten minutes." After-thoughts generally are not well received; neither are perceived attempts at manipulation.

If you notice that a set of materials looks great, use the thirty seconds it takes to say so on your way to the meeting or as you return. Also be specific; for instance, "The chart you prepared really helped me make my point." Mere pats on the back are not enough. Secretaries need to know their work has meaning and that their efforts make a difference in helping a boss accomplish goals.

Most important, reactions to your secretary's performance should be given directly to your secretary—not to others. Your secretary needs to know how you think things are going and needs to hear it from you in a timely manner.

Listening Effectively

The health of the communication relationship you share with your secretary depends on your making an effort to listen carefully to what your secretary is telling you. I use the term *listening* broadly to mean that you should, in fact, listen with more than your ears. You must learn how to read your secretary's behavior, not only noticing whether your secretary understands your directions, but also being aware of whether all is well or if something may be awry between the two of you.

A smart boss learns how to figure out what his or her secretary really means by what is said and how he or she truly feels about a situation by what is *not* said. Too many bosses don't look past the surface. You cannot afford to rely merely on what your secretary verbalizes to you. You must get beyond it and look for cues that reflect the true state of affairs. Take the extra few seconds required to notice how your secretary is reacting to things you say and do. You can learn more by watching your secretary's face as you give an assignment than you can in a 15-minute dialogue.

Here is a case in point: John, as a new program administrator in a training firm, experienced first-hand how important this rule is. John's boss, Suzanne, assigned a project to him and then called in her secretary, Jeanette, to instruct her to do the copying John required to complete the project. Jeanette smiled and said, "Sure, Suzanne," and left the room. However, upon leaving, Jeanette clearly revealed just how she felt about the assignment. She sighed deeply and her face fell just the slightest bit as she heard the assignment. And as she left the room, the smile, which had been noticeably tight in the first place, vanished and her eyes were on the floor. John did not miss this reaction. Suzanne, however, was already caught up looking at something on her desk and missed the entire display.

Not wanting to make an enemy of Jeanette the first week on the job, John took it upon himself to make his own copies and to set things straight between the two of them. He learned that Jeanette was overloaded with priority projects herself and felt it was unfair of Suzanne to load her with John's junk work. John certainly understood her position. Suzanne, however, was not a smart boss. By not taking the time to notice that things were not right with Jeanette, she allowed Jeanette's resentment to grow, inadvertently sabotaging her productivity. Unhappy secretaries do not put forth peak performance. The relationship deteriorated and Jeanette, an excellent secretary in all respects, finally resigned.

You can't solve problems unless you are aware that something is wrong. Don't be oblivious to your secretary's messages just because they are not blatantly obvious. Get to know your secretary's communication behavior and soon you will become adept at spotting irregularities that may reflect potential difficulties in your working relationship.

Further, don't assume your secretary is always being straight with you. Pick up on all nonverbal messages—everything about your secretary's communication outside the words themselves. Then if you think you detect a disparity between what is being said and what is displayed or if he or she says nothing at all, you can tactfully open the door to discussion.

Handling Conflict

There is a hard and fast rule about handling conflict in the secretary/manager relationship: *Talk to your secretary about your secretary.* It's as simple as that.

Don't complain to your friends or the personnel department when something is wrong, talk to your secretary directly. A friend in personnel often laments, "Why do they always come running to me whenever there's a problem? I can't understand why they can't just work it out between them." It's not as if most situations are so earth shattering as to require outside arbitration.

For example, Tom's secretary, Maureen, was habitually 10 to 15 minutes late each morning. It was very important to Tom that Maureen be at her desk first thing in the morning to answer the phones during what is their busiest time. When Maureen was not there on time, Tom's day started off all wrong. Tom was angry with Maureen before she even arrived, and Maureen couldn't understand why. Tom, unhappy about the situation, went to personnel to complain about Maureen.

Aside from her tardiness, Maureen happened to be one of the top secretaries in the company. She felt something was up with Tom because he was acting strangely. Personnel called Maureen in for a talk. This didn't do much for Maureen's morale. She felt insulted by such a petty complaint, especially since she often stayed well past quitting time to tie up things before leaving. In her mind, everything balanced out. Maureen sat and stewed.

Not only did Tom fail to solve his problem, he created a bigger one. Maureen's attitude toward the job and the company soured a little. If Maureen suspected that Tom instigated the scolding, it would have been all the worse for him. A wedge was driven between them that widened as time went by and similar situations occurred.

Had Tom gone directly to Maureen, we might have had a happy ending to this story. Assuming Maureen was a reasonable woman, Tom's explanation may well have made sense to her, neutralizing her reaction to the complaint as petty. Further, their relationship would have remained intact without the interference of an outside party and would even be strengthened as a result.

Certainly this example is a fairly uncomplicated situation. The fact is, most annoyances are of this same caliber. Small frustrations pile up and grow. That's why it's so important to nip small irritations in the bud. In the case of more complex problems, it's still the best idea to talk directly to your secretary to see if the two of you can't come up with workable strategies for rectifying the situation.

Confrontation is never easy. But considering the consequences of avoidance, it remains the wisest choice. In broaching problem situations with your secretary, the best tactic is to keep the mood light and try, if possible, to infuse humor into the conversation. Don't confront when you're angry, that will only stir up defenses. Get your point across and then allow your secretary to give his or her side of the story. Airing differences and then putting your heads together to seek solutions is a far better course than taking the problem to the outside.

You also must follow the converse of this rule: *Encourage your secretary to talk to you about you.* Put yourself on the line and find out what you do that drives him or her crazy. If your ego is strong enough to take it, following this rule will provide many benefits. Number one, you will get solutions to problem situations. Number two, the secretary/manager relationship will be strengthened. Number three, if your secretary feels free to come to you, it will curb participation in nonproductive coffee-klatch activities.

You remember the coffee klatch—it's where secretaries who do not share good relationships with managers spend a lot of time complaining about them. It's where secretaries get support for not cooperating with you. It's where poor attitudes are born and low standards of production are nurtured. This you don't need.

Inviting discussion, of course, requires the use of a non-threatening tone and a careful choice of words. Something like, "Carolyn, I have a feeling something is not quite right. Would you tell me what's up?" is an open expression of willingness to listen. On the other hand, "Carolyn, will you please stop moping around and tell me what's wrong?" may well evoke a defensive response.

When it comes to following this rule, only the first step is difficult. Once you and your secretary have opened dialogue concerning gripes you have about each other, future incidences become much easier to handle. By talking to each other about each other, you will take big steps toward becoming a tight team.

Secretary/Manager Communication Traps

The communication behavior of many secretaries reflects some of the occupational hazards of what it has historically meant to be a secretary. Since it takes at least two to form communication patterns, unenlightened managers often unwittingly fall into traps that can interfere with team development and negatively affect the work relationship. Understanding how the same factors that influence the relationship in other ways sometimes affect communication styles can help you overcome problems that might arise.

"Just a Secretary" Mindset

Some secretaries are intimidated when talking with managers. There is a subconscious feeling that being only a secretary means an individual somehow isn't as good as others within an organization. Such intimidation can turn into a fearful communication style. A secretary may withhold thoughts, questions, ideas, and suggestions, concluding that anything to be mentioned is only something you would already have thought of or, if not, is just not valuable. If you don't understand how a secretary feels, or worse, if you share a "just a secretary" mindset, you may wrongly assume your secretary has nothing to contribute. In this case, it's up to you to draw out the secretary.

On the other hand, you may have come up against secretaries who represent the opposite extreme. True professionals are fiercely proud of their profession. On the whole, they feel good about themselves and their work. But they may be angry, either consciously or unconsciously, because they think *you* don't recognize their importance. In this case *you* means not only you as an individual, but also you as a representative of management or the world in general. This can translate into defensive communication behavior. These secretaries can be hostile or ultrasensitive to any indication that a manager doesn't consider them professionals or equals.

It's up to you to recognize where defensiveness is coming from, to be sure you aren't unwittingly contributing to it, and to diffuse hostility before it destroys your relationship. Don't get caught up in hostile behavior—keep your cool. Get past defensive or hostile behavior by tactfully insisting your secretary explain rather than stew in silence so that solutions may be found to problem situations.

Underutilization and the Perception Gap

Another hazard of the average secretarial position that can negatively affect a secretary's communication behavior is having little practice in taking risks. If you think about it, secretaries often sit safely in a supporting role watching managers take all the chances. Many secretaries have been offered few, if any, opportunities to take risks in the normal course of day-to-day work and therefore rarely experience the boost of self-confidence that flows from taking chances and succeeding. As a result, many secretaries are afraid of taking risks in general and do not trust their own instincts. It may seem a monumental risk to a secretary to approach a manager directly, to be really open, or to share ideas. Many secretaries simply lack the confidence to talk to managers as equals. This can translate not only into a fearful communication style but, even worse, a silent one.

Low levels of self-confidence among secretaries also can be fed by a lack of understanding about the true nature of the secretary's function. As already mentioned, some secretaries don't have a clear understanding of how they really contribute to the operations of a department and an organization. Obviously, a person has to know the value of his or her work to feel good about it.

You can help build your secretary's confidence by your commitment to a contemporary point of view and by expressing your appreciation of the secretary's value. If you sense a secretary is holding back, draw out him or her.

Stereotyped Roles

A very common communication problem among many secretaries is a general nonassertiveness. The reasons behind this communication style are more complex than might be readily apparent. Sometimes individual personality has something to do with nonassertiveness. It is also a throwback to a sexual stereotype of women that existed before the feminist movement, and of course, it is still true that most secretaries are women. While assertiveness training has been popular for a long time, training programs aimed at secretaries are only now becoming widespread.

Experience has shown, however, that problems with assertiveness are not simply tied to the individual secretary, but rather have more to do with the overall secretary/manager relationship. Years ago, the secretary/manager relationship was governed by then-accepted dominant/submissive, male/female roles, because it was generally true that bosses were men and secretaries were women. While it's safe to say that society is moving away from applying specific roles to men and women, the effect of stereotyped roles still lingers in the secretary/manager relationship. Maybe it has something to do with the fact that the secretary is the subordinate. This surely doesn't make it any easier to break out of the submissive role. One can be assertive without crossing the line into insubordination, though.

In any event, the assertiveness problem is connected to how the secretarial role is perceived. In professional-development workshops conducted by the author, participants share with one another how they would handle given problem situations at the office. A typical scenario involves the secretary taking on many added responsibilities and asking the boss for a change in title and a raise.

Initially, each participant is asked in a round-table discussion to explain to the group how he or she would handle the situation. Participants generally are authoritative and articulate in stating their case and appear confident of their ability to persuade a manager to see their point of view.

Next, two volunteers are asked to role play the situation, with one as manager and the other as secretary. As the role playing begins, it is immediately apparent that there is a big difference in how the manager and secretary behave. The secretary speaks softly, often inaudibly, slouches noticeably in the chair, cannot maintain meaningful eye contact, displays nervous gestures, and generally comes across as meek and fearful. The boss, on the other hand, sits tall and straight, speaks in a strong if not booming voice, is articulate, and also is noticeably impatient with the whining secretary.

Next, the volunteers switch roles. The meek and mild secretary suddenly becomes the assertive boss and vice versa. By now the rest of the workshop participants are aching for the opportunity to show the others how to do it right. But each team exhibits the same behavior.

The inescapable truth is that the secretaries' communication behavior reflects an unconscious acceptance of the submissive nature of the secretarial role. Not until actually faced with the audience's candid reaction to each participant's behavior does each participant see that it is true—secretaries themselves are influenced by an outdated perspective of their role.

Obviously, a secretary who is unconsciously trapped in the submissive role has a limited ability to contribute as a full-fledged member of the organizational team. That means it's up to you to work to overcome this built-in problem.

Recognize the potential influence of stereotyping on your secretary's communication style. Make it a point to look beyond superficial behavior to discover what your secretary is really like. Be careful not to unwittingly encourage your secretary to maintain stereotypical behaviors. Speak to your secretary as an equal—don't be patronizing. Don't play into attempts to cast you in the dominant role, challenge your secretary to think independently and to express personal views to you. Encourage your secretary to rely on personal judgment rather than to depend on you for continual reassurance. Show your willingness to take the time to discuss what your secretary considers important.

Coffee-Klatch Influence

Finally, there are those secretaries whose behavior is strongly influenced by other secretaries in a company—enter again the coffee-klatch syndrome. As discussed in Chapter 1, secretaries firmly entrenched in an organizational coffee klatch sometimes exhibit a general unwillingness to be open and honest with managers because they are considered the enemy. In this case, it's up to you to let a secretary know he or she is accepted as a member of your team. Your acceptance provides the courage and reassurance a secretary needs to separate from the pack.

Overall

It takes two people to form a communication pattern. If the communication behavior of one party is altered, the other cannot help but change too in order to reach a new equilibrium. If you take the initiative in ensuring that your communication style reflects a contemporary view of your secretary, your secretary will certainly grow in response.

Through your communication behavior, continually reinforce the fact that you consider your secretary a valuable part of your team. You can have a positive impact on how your secretary feels about himself or herself and the job, improving your communication and team effectiveness. The payoff will be well worth the effort.

CHAPTER FIVE

KEEPING YOUR SECRETARY HAPPY

What Do Secretaries Really Want?

Once you've hired a really top-notch assistant, the trick is to hold on to that person. What does it take to keep a secretary happy? Secretaries basically want three things:

☐ Participation as a team member.

☐ Recognition for their contribution.

☐ Compensation appropriate to their contribution.

All three are critical, yet compensation is probably the most significant, because money symbolizes all that's traditionally been wrong with being a secretary. It's a reflection of being overlooked and undervalued. But, while money is a big issue, it's not the only barrier between a secretary and job satisfaction.

We really are talking about the whole issue of motivation. Of course, a motivated secretary is the key to a successful, productive secretary/manager relationship. So far, you already will have picked up many cues as to how to motivate your secretary. Maintaining an overall perspective of the secretary as a valuable, contributing member of your work team goes a long way toward ensuring your secretary's continuing contentment. To recap, here are actions we've already discussed that display your commitment to a modern view:

Fully utilize your secretary's skills, talents, and abilities:

☐ Recognize the difference between technical and discretionary skills.

☐ Identify your secretary's particular abilities and special talents.

☐ Delegate work that takes advantage of your secretary's capabilities.

Encourage your secretary's creativity and professional growth:

☐ Seek your secretary's ideas, suggestions, and opinions.

☐ Provide opportunities for training.

☐ Allow your secretary to practice newly learned skills.

119

Communicate:

☐ Tell your secretary what he or she needs to know.

☐ Provide meaningful feedback.

☐ Dare to confide.

These behaviors convey to secretaries that they are considered a part of the team. They also indirectly indicate that a secretary's contributions are considered valuable. Later in the chapter we will discuss more good boss behaviors that will keep your secretary happy. But first, let's tackle the big issue—secretarial compensation.

Compensation—The No. 1 Issue

Secretaries and salaries—an area where it's going to take a lot to set things straight. Secretaries have some legitimate complaints in this area, and secretarial compensation issues are complex. Here is some background.

Despite the growing shortage of qualified candidates, the law of supply and demand has not significantly increased secretarial salary levels for a variety of reasons. According to E. James Brennan, a pay-practice consultant and recognized expert on secretarial compensation with Brennan, Thomsen Associates of St. Louis, Missouri, one difficulty is the lack of a consistent definition of the secretary's duties. Another is the desperate or marginal candidate who accepts a lower-than-appropriate salary just to get a foot in the door. Then there's the organization that lowers its standards, thereby justifying low salary levels, rather than spending the time and money to attract and retain hard-to-find qualified secretaries. The bottom line is that supply and demand establish a minimum threshold for secretarial pay below which you can't hire anyone. Above the threshold, Brennan says, "it's complete anarchy."

What rules secretarial salaries above market minimum level, according to Brennan, are an organization's internal priorities governing the secretarial skills it values and how managers are encouraged to utilize their secretaries. Brennan believes that 80 percent of secretarial compensation issues could be resolved if companies were consistent about the parameters of secretarial jobs. A professional secretary would add that if an agreed-upon standard doesn't reflect an enlightened view, however, it still would be unfair and inaccurate even if it *were* consistent.

As was mentioned in Chapter 1, many companies do not even have job descriptions for secretaries, let alone determine salaries according to in-depth job analysis. Accepted pay practice dictates that salaries should be tied to the officially designated duties of a position and to their performance. Yet secretarial pay usually is determined by the title of the boss, not by the value of the job duties and the contribution of the individual.

To top things off (and it's no surprise), secretarial salaries remain low because the profession is female-dominated. Brennan believes that social custom and economic history prove that a job performed by a woman still is perceived as less valuable than a similar job done by a man.

Secretarial pay scales and practices aren't going to significantly improve overnight, and you alone can't do anything to change that fact. There are, however, ways you can help ensure that money issues will not come between you and your secretary.

Your first concern (if you have control or at least influence over setting salary) is that the salary you offer is competitive within your geographic area, industry, and type of company. It's difficult to provide specific guidelines for secretarial salaries because of significant geographic differences and the fact that any figures quoted could change so rapidly. Generally, however, the larger the sales revenues and profits of an employer and the larger the metropolitan area, the higher the pay.

Certain industries traditionally pay secretaries at different levels: for example, advertising, retailing, banking, entertainment, fashion, cosmetic, and other glamour fields tend to pay lower salaries; transportation, utilities, manufacturing, financial, legal, and consulting firms pay on the higher end of the spectrum. The higher the inherent reward or prestige of working in the industry, the lower the pay.

To compare the salary you offer with the general marketplace, start with the help-wanted section of your local newspaper. Also, area wage surveys are often available, and a local chapter of Professional Secretaries International (see Appendix) may provide competitive data. A reliable recruiter also can provide guidance on what constitutes a competitive salary in your situation.

A big part of determining salary requires you to understand the value of the particular job. Brennan recommends that a manager who wants to ensure that a secretary is being appropriately compensated should determine how much would be paid to a man with the same credentials doing the same type of work (excluding transcription) in terms of span of control, the ability to operate independently, set schedules, monitor and control the executive's time, and to act as proxy in the executive's absence.

Ask the questions: "What is the value added to the executive's effectiveness by the secretary? How much is it worth to the organization?" If the answer is a salary that is considered too high for a highly qualified secretary, then ask, "Can the organization afford a secretary who requires such close supervision or has such limited abilities that it's going to take even more of the executive's time rather than help better utilize it?" Or, "Isn't it worth an appropriate salary to hire someone qualified to free up the executive to better accomplish his or her goals?"

Finally, you must deal with how your own value system meshes with that of your company. A problem can arise when you hire a highly qualified secretary and find that you are restricted from paying an appropriate salary because you are using the secretary beyond the company's expected standard. This, of course, can translate into a secretary who is thrilled with the work but becomes unhappy, frustrated, and ultimately, bitter and angry about the salary.

It's important that you know what your company endorses as the standard duties of a secretarial position, to understand its limits, and to know how much a secretary can do above and beyond those limits for it to be considered the same job. Making this clear to a secretary right off the bat can head off later trouble resulting from an imbalance of expectations.

A secretary wants a competitive salary that accurately reflects the value of his or her capabilities, experience, responsibilities, and job performance. Do your best to provide just that. If your hands are tied because of situations beyond your control, there are ways to work around the problem. Read on for ideas that can help you beat the money issue.

A Broad View of Compensation—Perks and Privileges

A secretary is motivated to work hard for a boss who cares that he or she is appropriately compensated. Take an active part in determining how your company will remunerate your secretary in terms of salary and other benefits. Do your best to ensure that your secretary receives the maximum you believe he or she is entitled to, according to his or her value to you.

Negotiate on your secretary's behalf for raises or other benefits (examples of which follow) and fight for what you consider appropriate—don't just make casual recommendations. Even if you don't always succeed, your effort shows that your secretary's satisfaction matters to you and will go a long way in building good will.

If, as already discussed, you are kept from providing what you consider an appropriate salary, try to win other benefits from the company to make up the difference. If your company fails to come through, think about judiciously providing benefits out of your own pocket. Consider it an investment in your career and find creative ways to make up for a less-than-satisfactory salary.

If it is appropriate in your company setting, you can simply supplement your secretary's salary in cash. Some bosses call it a wardrobe allowance. Periodic cash bonuses are another way to go and can be even more effective if timed carefully, such as at times other than holidays, in recognition of work anniversaries, or upon completion of a particularly difficult assignment.

Bonuses don't have to be in cash; your situation may be better suited to other kinds of supplements. A secretary may have an eye on something you can pay for. Take the case of Karen. Karen and her boss, Ann, had just finished putting together a large client presentation that required working late for more than a week. When the project was completed, Ann told Karen she wanted to do something to show her appreciation, but didn't know what would please Karen most. A leather briefcase had caught Karen's eye earlier that week and she mentioned it to Ann. Ann said, "Go pick it up for yourself on me."

Perhaps you have access to perks through your work or personal life that you can extend to your secretary. One attorney who represents the owner of a major theater chain shares with his secretary access to prime theater tickets that are available on a moment's notice through the client. Another manager whose husband was in the travel business was able to extend travel discounts to her secretary. If you think about it, you're sure to come up with something of value to which you have easy access that can be extended to your secretary.

One valuable perk that not only benefits your secretary, but you and your company as well, is payment of membership dues to a professional association, such as Professional Secretaries International (PSI). Many secretaries complain they want to take part in professional organizations and related events but can't afford to. Professional associations provide many avenues for supplementing a secretary's salary. In addition to covering membership dues, you or your company can pay for your secretary's monthly dinner meetings, registration and travel expenses to conferences and conventions, and fees for seminars and other events sponsored by the association.

Sponsorship in an organization that serves to further professional growth and development provides you with a valuable payback and also conveys a belief in your secretary's professionalism, which is one of your primary goals as a modern boss. Point out to management the value of sponsoring membership for your secretary and perhaps all the secretaries in the firm—this is a prime benefit worth fighting for.

If your secretary isn't ready to make a commitment to an organization, you could pay for a subscription to a professional journal, such as *The Secretary,* or one of the many other newsletters published for secretaries, such as *The Personal Report for the Professional Secretary,* published by The National Institute of Business Management. Your secretary probably receives frequent mailings about such newsletters and other programs and services directed to secretaries if you need other ideas.

Another valued perk rarely offered to secretaries is compensatory time off. If your secretary has been working above and beyond the call of duty, offer a long weekend, an afternoon off, or an extended lunch hour and don't charge the time to official vacation or personal time off. Use your discretionary power. Allow flexibility in working hours when possible. An extra hour in the morning or an occasional short afternoon is very much appreciated by secretaries who usually work by the clock, unlike most other people in the office. Compensatory time off is especially appreciated when the secretary doesn't have to ask for it. Take the initiative and offer—it's a more effective motivator that way.

Giving Recognition and Showing Appreciation

Outside of compensation, recognition and appreciation are the big two with secretaries. When it comes to recognition, think small. Giving recognition doesn't have to mean banquets, speeches, and honors bestowed. In fact, going overboard with good intentions can backfire because professional secretaries react negatively to patronizing. Recognition should occur on a regular basis, not wait until an annual review or Professional Secretaries Day. One secretary, Carolyn, describes why she was so satisfied working with one former boss:

> He was generous with praise, always gave recognition and credit to those who earned it, and always backed up his praise with monetary compensation and/or promotions when the time came. Hal always introduced me to his business associates and colleagues and gave me recognition in front of them for work I had prepared for their meetings. In return, he almost never had to ask me to stay late or come in on a weekend. When it was apparent to me that he needed me, I would approach him to ask whether he needed me to stay. I was rarely ill during the years I worked with him, and I think a lot of this has to do with contentment.

Seemingly small gestures, such as being introduced to clients and associates as Carolyn mentioned, help fulfill a secretary's need for recognition. Being personally informed of the outcome of projects also is important. If your secretary has worked with you on a long, difficult project, don't let him or her hear of its consequence third-hand or by accident—give the news yourself. Also make sure you include your secretary in a project's wrap-up meetings or celebrations, whether they be preplanned parties or spur-of-the-moment gatherings in your office. Of course, always remember to give credit where credit is due. Recognize your secretary's contribution to a project in front of people who count.

You need to show appreciation of all your secretary does for you, especially for special favors not considered and agreed on in advance as part of the job, such as running personal errands, volunteering to work through lunch, coming in early, or staying late.

When it comes to recognition and appreciation, good intentions easily can and often do go awry. You can get into trouble by forgetting that you are a modern boss and reverting to inappropriate thank-yous better saved for personal relationships: sending a card, buying flowers or candy, or taking your secretary out to lunch. To the professional secretary, this is much like men holding doors open for feminist activists.

Appreciation means more than just saying "thank you." Refer back to the guidelines for providing meaningful feedback discussed in Chapter 4 and also to the section in this chapter on perks for secretaries for appropriate ways to show your appreciation. Above all, don't wait until Professional Secretaries Day to recognize your secretary. If you use and abuse your secretary all year and think you can make things right on this one day, you're bound for trouble.

Don't Forget Professional Secretaries Week®

The dilemma of how to appropriately show appreciation becomes particularly acute during Professional Secretaries Week. It's hard to know what to do, especially when you are bombarded with advertisements emphasizing the card and flowers approach. It's true, some secretaries are happy with this sort of gesture. Usually any attention at all is welcome because they feel so overlooked. If you come across secretaries who are that far behind the times, however, do them a favor and enlighten them.

It's good for you to understand what Professional Secretaries Day and Professional Secretaries Week are really all about.[1] National Secretaries Week, as it was originally called, was initiated

[1]Professional Secretaries Day and Professional Secretaries Week are trademarks of Professional Secretaries International.

in 1952 by the president of the National Secretaries Association (now known as PSI) and the president of Dictaphone Corporation, who were working on a council to address the national shortage of skilled office workers.

The two approached the secretary of commerce, Charles Sawyer, about proclaiming a National Secretaries Week with the purpose of recognizing ". . .the American secretary, upon whose skills, loyalty, and efficiency the functions of business and government depend." The objective was to call attention "through favorable publicity, to the tremendous potential of the secretarial career." Somewhere along the way, the card and flower industry caught hold and turned an attempt to gain recognition into just another hearts and flowers holiday.

Professional secretaries are pleased to see, however, that in recent years attention to the day has taken on a more contemporary tenor, focusing on the challenges faced by secretaries and the organizations they serve in the information age and the automated office.

To the true professional secretary, the purpose of Professional Secretaries Week is to draw attention to the fact that it's time to take a contemporary perspective of the secretary and to give up, once and for all, the secretarial stereotype. Many hope that in the not-too-distant future, Professional Secretaries Week will no longer be needed because there will no longer be a stereotype to fight.

What is an appropriate way to mark these events? Your best bet is to watch for what's going on in your area that reflects the intended spirit of the day and week.

Local chambers of commerce often sponsor some type of luncheon awards event in which area companies are invited to participate. A recent trend has been the combination benefit and recognition lunch or dinner, such as the "All Star Salute to Secretaries" put on jointly by chapters of the Arthritis Foundation and Professional Secretaries International.

Many seminars also are offered during the week. One example is the American Management Association's "Seminar by Satellite" videoconference, in which secretaries in cities across the country simultaneously participate in a program in honor of the day. If you pay attention to the mail that crosses your desk during the few weeks prior to Professional Secretaries Week, you certainly will get some good ideas.

Even if you are unable to attend such an event with your secretary, you can still send him or her to a seminar or other event not specifically for both secretary and boss. A good example is a biannual event sponsored by Professional Secretaries International called "Secretary Speakout." At Speakout events, secretaries from all over the country gather to discuss and reach a consensus statement on a topic relevant to the profession. You can obtain information on Speakout and other events being sponsored by PSI in your area by calling PSI headquarters in Kansas City at (816) 531-7010.

Even if your company routinely recognizes all its secretaries in honor of the week, you still must do something for your own secretary. This is especially true where the company chooses a less-than-professional approach (as is often the case) and gives each secretary a plant or something else inappropriate.

The personnel director of one large law firm was pleased to have approval from management to spend much more money than the usual budgeted amount (as a result of intensive persuasion and persistence) for tokens of appreciation in honor of Professional Secretaries Week. Expensive candy was purchased (not a recommended choice and not much of an improvement over the usual plant). To each package was attached a personally typed note of appreciation from "management."

While some secretaries believed the choice of candy was inappropriate, overall reception of the gesture was very positive. Why? Not because of the candy, but because of the personally typed and signed notes. *That* was what mattered most—that someone cared enough to type and sign a note of appreciation just for each secretary.

An unfortunate result was that many of the attorneys apparently assumed that since management was taking care of these gifts, they didn't have to do anything themselves in honor of the week. Some didn't even mention it. Remember the point already discussed: What matters most to secretaries is how they are treated by their own managers. A secretary wants you to remember and recognize Professional Secretaries Week or Day.

As already said, not all secretaries are enlightened; many want gifts in honor of the day. From a professional's point of view, attending a seminar or other appropriate event is highly preferable to gifts, but if gift buying is the norm in your company, it's all right to go along so long as the gift reflects professionalism. Here are some gift suggestions for a wide range of budgets:

☐ Subscription to a professional journal or serious magazine such as *The Secretary* or *Working Woman.*

☐ Quality pen and pencil set.

☐ Desk outfit—blotter, pen holder, etc.

☐ Leather organizer or calendar.

☐ Attaché case or leather tote bag.

☐ Reimbursement of fees for a course or seminar that will further your secretary's professional growth.

☐ Membership dues in a professional association.

☐ Reimbursement of expenses for a conference, convention, exhibition, or other event relevant to your industry or the secretarial profession.

Mark Professional Secretaries Week (the last full week in April) and Professional Secretaries Day (Wednesday of that week) on your calendar. Until the time comes when we all look back on this time and laugh to ourselves that it was necessary to single out secretaries in order that they be recognized and appreciated, it's very important for you to remember Professional Secretaries Week. No matter how you choose to honor your secretary, don't let those important dates pass unnoticed.

Good Boss Behaviors

Here are more guidelines for building a successful relationship with your secretary.

Between You and Your Secretary

Explaining Decisions. Whenever possible, give your secretary background to the decisions you've made so he or she can better understand and identify with them. If you decide that your secretary can't take off a certain week for vacation, for example, explain your reasoning. Simply laying down the law will only make your secretary feel like a child with you as parent—precisely opposite from the team experience you're trying to create.

This also applies to decisions that come down from upper management. If you're aware of the rationale behind rulings mandated from above, share the background with your secretary. This will nip in the bud negativism about the decision as well as eliminate the effects of grapevine guessing as to what's going on.

To go even a step further, include your secretary in decisions that involve him or her. It is, of course, well-accepted management philosophy that participating in decision making means better acceptance of and compliance with decisions.

Respecting Privacy.   Secretaries and privacy are two words that don't go together very well. Lack of privacy is an occupational hazard for secretaries because of the way most offices are set up. Notice that most secretaries sit at a desk out in the open somewhere close to the manager's office. Sometimes there are makeshift cubicles or other efforts made to provide a somewhat closed environment for the secretary, but rarely do secretaries have their own offices.

Being left out in the open makes secretaries vulnerable to continual observation by others and creates a lack of privacy that can be very disturbing. No one enjoys working with someone looking over his or her shoulder. If your secretary is situated just outside your door, arrange your desk so that you are not looking right out at him or her. Do whatever you can within your space limitations to provide your secretary with as much privacy as possible.

One of the problems that results from being out in the open is that secretaries often are almost too available. Someone who has an office has the option of closing the door. Even if the door is open, visitors are expected to knock before entering. But a secretary's desk is all too easy to approach. A secretary in this situation tends to feel exposed, vulnerable, and generally uncomfortable. Many secretaries complain that even if they're on the phone, people just walk up and stand there listening to the conversation, waiting for the call to end or, worse, interrupt the phone conversation. This is boldly rude behavior, but it happens all the time.

One secretary had a painfully amusing story to tell that illustrates how a lack of privacy can turn into continual frustration. Laurie's desk is situated out in the open. She complains that people think nothing of walking right up to her desk and interrupting her for the silliest things. One day a manager approached as Laurie was busy working on a document and interrupted her to ask her where her out box was. The out box was right behind Laurie with a 12- by 3-inch bright yellow sign with OUT BOX posted above it. To a secretary, this kind of behavior reflects an attitude that says it's okay to interrupt secretaries because what they do isn't very important.

Whether your own setup is particularly good or bad, there are ways you can help the situation. For one thing, don't run out to your secretary's desk every time you think of something to say, ask, or assign. If you have an intercom, use it. But use the intercom wisely. If you can see that your secretary is on the phone, allow a minute or two for the call to be ended. If time goes on and the call doesn't end, call on the intercom or slip a note asking your secretary to see you when he or she is free.

Further, respect your secretary's space. Don't touch things on his or her desk or go through drawers or files unless you have express permission to do so. Secretaries who walk up to find someone standing at their desk feel like their privacy has been invaded, just as the manager who walks into his or her office to find someone sitting at the desk or looking through papers on a credenza.

Staying Out of the Way. Here's another situation that is complicated by a secretary's overavailability. Once you've assigned certain projects to your secretary, for heaven's sake, leave him or her alone as much as possible to do the work. If you've clearly explained what you want done, there's no need to keep checking up. As you're giving initial instructions, be sure to tell your secretary to come to you with questions or problems. Then trust him or her to follow through. This is not to say you shouldn't be allowed to ask for progress reports. Find a comfortable medium—don't run out every 10 minutes and ask, "Is it finished yet?"

Secretaries don't enjoy working with bosses who are constantly underfoot. Don't continually impose your presence on your secretary. Many managers are unconsciously in the way. In one office, this was a continual problem between June, the manager, and Cathy, her secretary. The managers' mail in this office was distributed to the desk of each manager's secretary. The secretaries' desks in this office were designed with a chest-high partition at the front with a foot-wide ledge on top—ironically to provide the secretary with a little privacy. June had a habit of coming out to look at her mail, which was stacked on the ledge at the front of Cathy's desk.

June would open, sort, and read her mail while standing at Cathy's desk, violating her privacy and causing her anxiety. As she read the mail, she'd reach onto Cathy's desk for a paper clip, a pencil, the stapler, the Rolodex file for a number, and even the phone to make a call. Further, June would make comments to Cathy about whatever she was reading, distracting her from the work she was trying to get done. Then she'd go into her office and ask, "Is that letter done yet?"

Clearly, June's behavior was unconscious. Make sure you're not thoughtlessly doing something that keeps your secretary from accomplishing his or her work. In short, stay out of the way.

Giving the Benefit of the Doubt.   We touched on this area in connection with trust, but it bears repeating as a good boss behavior. Remember that your secretary is on your side. If there's really a problem, talk about it. But don't jump to conclusions about your secretary's behavior.

If it seems your secretary is on the phone a great deal, don't automatically assume you're being taken advantage of. People often think that whenever a secretary is on the phone, the call is personal. A lot of the secretary's work happens to be conducted by telephone. Yes, secretaries sometimes do make personal calls, but they're not alone. In any event, it doesn't necessarily mean that the privilege is being abused.

Always think before you approach. If you feel you must intervene, inquire—don't accuse. For example, say you've asked your secretary to summarize a stack of reports for your committee meeting. The meeting is to be held at 3:00 P.M., it's now 1:00 P.M., you haven't received the summary, and your secretary is standing at the desk of another secretary talking.

Number one, don't assume what they're talking about is personal. It may be, it may not. Second, don't take the attitude that regardless of what they're talking about, what you have to say is more important. Secretaries often complain about being treated as lesser human beings, and this is an often-cited case in point. Give your secretary the chance to prove he or she is capable of meeting deadlines and managing time without your intervention. What should matter is results, not methods.

Following Through on Promises.   If you say you're going to do something, do it. Just because you haven't used the word *promise* doesn't mean this rule doesn't apply. Here are some common areas where secretaries complain their bosses have let them down:

□ "We'll go through that pile of paper this week."

□ "We'll talk about your vacation tomorrow."

□ "I'll look into ordering you a new typewriter tomorrow."

□ "I'll talk to the supervisor about your raise/promotion/ title change next week."

□ "We'll talk about your request to handle more projects soon."

□ "You'll have some time off as soon as things calm down."

□ "Give me a proposal on that idea and I'll consider it."

□ "Put that proposal in writing and I'll take it to my supervisor."

□ "We'll review your proposal to hire a part-time assistant at the beginning of next week."

□ "If we get this account, I'll see that you get a bonus for your efforts."

□ "This is the last time I'll interrupt you today."

Many secretaries have difficulty reminding a boss of what he or she promised to do. Just because you don't hear about it doesn't mean your secretary has forgotten what you said. More than likely, he or she is stewing over the fact that time continues to go by without your action. Frustration builds, attitudes sour, and the relationship can start down the tubes.

If you are unable to act within a given time frame, at least give your secretary an indication that you're aware of the situation, that you intend to follow through, and that you have a plan for dealing with it.

Reciprocating Favors.   The boss who takes the "we're equals" rather than a "me king, you slave" approach is best accepted by secretaries. Find ways to reciprocate favors your secretary does for you. For instance, Susan regularly did Jim's banking, something which wasn't in Susan's job description and that saved Jim a lot of time. Since time was the issue, Jim thought of ways in which he could repay Susan with time—such as offering her extra time at lunch on payday to do her own banking.

Showing an Interest.   A common complaint of secretaries is that they are treated like nonpersons. Remember that a secretary is not there just for you to order around. Don't shut out your secretary.

A secretary will feel left out, for instance, to hear through a third party that you closed on a new house. And a secretary will feel put out if he or she's the star on the company softball team and you never ask how the team did the night before.

It can be difficult to determine just how far one should go in showing an interest. You do need to find a business and personal balance in the relationship. On one hand, it is important for you to show a genuine interest in your secretary's activities outside of work, but then again, going too far in discussing personal lives could undermine the professionalism of your relationship.

You should definitely take an interest, for example, in anything your secretary does on the outside to further his or her professional growth and development, such as seminars, evening classes, or association memberships. Some personal interest is appropriate too, however. Take five minutes, for example, on Monday morning to find out how the weekend was. Not that you should sit through a play-by-play account of every activity, but at least get a rundown on the overall experience. This will not only show interest, but also give you a clue as to your secretary's state of mind on Monday morning. On Friday afternoon, casually ask whether anything special is planned for the weekend. Again, don't encourage too much detail; just show you realize there is life outside the office.

It is appropriate to be aware of your secretary's family situation in general as well as any special family problems, such as illness or difficult situations with children or other family members. You should not, however, be subjected to detailed daily reports. A brief inquiry as to how well things are going is enough. Stay away from getting too specific or being drawn in as a counselor or advisor. Your interest shows concern; your keeping out of specific problems shows you respect his or her ability to handle the situation.

Show human consideration, but don't be taken advantage of. If your secretary is too willing to provide more information than you care to hear, tactfully bring the conversation around to a work-related topic. He or she eventually will pick up on your cue.

Draw the line when it comes to your respective romantic lives and discussions concerning finances. Remember that although you work closely together, you are above all else the boss, not a friend. You should be friendly, but developing a real friendship can interfere with the superior/subordinate nature of the relationship.

Successfully striking a business and personal balance in your relationship can create an effective tightness about your team. Showing an interest can not only strengthen your relationship, but serve as yet another weapon in fighting off the coffee klatch in its attempts to draw your secretary into its camp. Remember, if your secretary feels isolated, he or she will head in that direction. All it takes on your part is a few well-chosen words to show you know a secretary is a person, too.

A Secretary's Pet Peeves

This will summarize the flip side of good boss behaviors in case you need a quick reference for comparing your behavior.

Interruptions.　Granted, to some degree it's the nature of the secretary's job to be at the whim of the boss; after all, secretarial work in large measure depends on the momentary needs of the manager. But remember to use good judgment—restrain yourself from needlessly or inappropriately interrupting your secretary as he or she tries to complete work assignments.

Procrastination.　We have said that it is all right to be a procrastinator as long as you admit it to your secretary. That doesn't mean secretaries like procrastination—in fact, they really hate it. If you are a procrastinator, at least force yourself to tell your secretary what work assignments you should be tackling and their respective deadlines so he or she can keep after you to get on it. And, there is a way to be considerate about your procrastination. Secretaries appreciate being warned well in advance if a serious work crunch is approaching so they may prepare for it, both mentally and in terms of juggling other work assignments.

Disorganization.   In general, secretaries by nature are organized people who dislike disorganization. But it's okay if you're disorganized though, because part of a secretary's job is to organize you. The key is to allow your secretary to do just that. Religiously conform with whatever systems and controls your secretary institutes to keep you organized. And apologize profusely when you're occasionally out of organizational control.

Inconsistency.   Do what you say you're going to do. And be predictable in work-related matters. A secretary needs to know how a boss will react in order to anticipate needs and act in the boss's absence.

Disloyalty.   Stand up for your secretary when the need arises. Good bosses never say anything about secretaries in their absence that they wouldn't say in their presence.

Isolation.   Don't overlook, ignore, or shut out your secretary.

Condescension.   There's no excuse for this one.

Being Taken for Granted.   Never take your secretary or anyone else for granted. Recognize and appreciate your secretary *every* day, not just on Professional Secretaries Day.

The Office Picture

What's it like for a secretary to work for your company? Chapter 1 discussed at length common organizational practices that are less than desirable from a secretary's point of view. More than likely, your company is guilty of at least a few of the infractions mentioned. Since you want a satisfied secretary, it's in your best interest to ensure that your secretary is protected from organizational mishandling.

Secretaries today are encouraged to be assertive in going after what they want from a company, yet experience shows that a secretary usually gets nowhere without a boss's support, especially in a company that still seems to be in the dark ages. It's up to you to use your influence, make up for shortcomings, and get around roadblocks in the system for your secretary's benefit. Don't forget, it's for your benefit too—secretaries are very loyal to and motivated to work hard for bosses who go to bat on their behalf.

To recap, the main areas where companies fall short include:

☐ Appropriate compensation.

☐ Properly distinguishing secretarial positions.

☐ Recognizing individual contributions of secretaries.

☐ Offering opportunity for career advancement.

☐ Generally drawing secretaries in as a true part of the organization.

Here are some suggestions for bridging the gap between what your company offers and what your secretary wants and needs.

The second and third items are closely related and stem from the whole area of secretarial stereotyping and the perception gap discussed in Chapter 1. An overly vague title or classification that doesn't accurately reflect the nature of your secretary's job may become a problem, especially when your secretary has reached the salary ceiling of the classification.

Your secretary will need not only your support to fight for a reclassification or change in title, but hard evidence as well. The solution goes back to a large part of the problem. Most companies do not have accurate job descriptions for secretaries, if they have them at all. Have your secretary create a job description for the position.

Creating a Job Description

Valid job descriptions result from in-depth job analysis, not from merely sitting down and writing a list of duties from memory. Three steps must be followed: data collection, analysis, and summary. You can't get to step three without first following through on steps one and two, especially when it comes to secretarial work (remember the influence of the stereotype and the perception gap).

If you're starting completely from scratch with no job description, valid or not, you might want to refer to the prototype secretarial job description that has been prepared by Professional Secretaries International (see Appendix). The prototype can be modified to suit your specific situation using the same process outlined here:

Step 1: Data Collection. Have your secretary keep a detailed log of daily activities. Entries should be made into this daily journal faithfully for a minimum of one month, preferably two. The object is to record every move that's made in the course of a day. Here are the rules:

□ Record everything—including the most trivial activities.

□ Be specific—don't just write down "answered the phone," but include who called and the outcome of the conversation, for example.

□ Pay close attention to communications of all kinds, oral and written, including names.

□ Make entries as you work—don't wait until later because you won't remember what you did. This is important.

Your secretary should be instructed not to read over the journal until at least a month, preferably two, has passed. Reading a few days' or even two weeks' worth of notes won't tell much. But over a good length of time, definite patterns will emerge.

Step 2: Analysis. The next step is to carefully review the journals and categorize activities. If possible, it's helpful if you and your secretary do this step together. It's also helpful to read completely through the journal pages a couple of times in order to process the information before attempting the actual categorizing. The categories themselves should make themselves evident. Here are some examples to help get started:

□ Office administration.

□ Client development.

□ Client relations.

□ Document drafting, editing, proofreading, or abstracting.

□ Financial.

□ Information management.

□ Meeting arrangement or preparation.

□ Project work.

□ Research.

□ Travel arrangement or preparation.

Start with a readily apparent category and search for all journal entries that apply. Work with one or two categories at a time, rather than going through line by line and attempting to assign each to a category. As an entry is assigned to a category, check it off.

Step 3: Summary.   Once the material is categorized, the final step is to put the information into logical order. Group related categories together and list duties and responsibilities in order of priority or however you deem appropriate. Additional sections may be added as an overall job summary indicating how the position fits into the department, to whom the secretary reports, others who are supported besides the principal managers, and the equipment the secretary uses. Your secretary's job description is finished.

You may wonder whether all this effort is worth the risk of opening this can of worms. It is possible, of course, that management will pay no attention at all to the new job description. Make it clear to your secretary from the start that the job description won't guarantee the desired results. In any event, the process offers many other benefits to secretaries and bosses.

First, secretaries very often gain a new respect for their job, because they have, maybe for the first time, a true understanding of how their work affects the boss's, the department's, and the company's goals. An accurate job description also can serve as a springboard for more effective use of secretaries and the development of untapped potential. Coordinating effort and expanding responsibilities take on new meaning when you have a solid base from which to start.

The job description also can prove invaluable in the performance appraisal process, the next area where you can positively influence your secretary's experience within your company.

The Performance Appraisal

Secretaries, like all other employees, anticipate that evaluation time of year. This is not only because appraisal time often is also raise time, although that certainly is a factor, but because they look forward to a meaningful discussion with their bosses about how they're doing and what's in the cards for them in the coming year. Don't let down your secretary in this important area. If your company's evaluation practices are unsatisfactory to the secretary, his or her frustration and poor attitude will focus on you. Here is some insight into what often goes wrong and guidelines for ensuring your secretary's appraisal experience is a fair and positive one.

The object of employee evaluation is to measure performance against expected standards. As already discused, the first obvious problem in appraising secretarial performance is that there usually is no accurate job description against which to compare a secretary. Another problem is that a large part of what a secretary does is not easily measurable. It's therefore hard to be objective, which is the goal of modern evaluation techniques.

Make Sure the Evaluation Isn't Overly General.   An appraisal can't be effective if it doesn't cover what is actually done on the job. A fair evaluation must look into the specific duties of the individual secretary's job. The evaluation shouldn't focus only on the technical aspects of the job, such as typing and dictation speed and accuracy, just because they are more readily apparent. Discretionary skills must be included in the evaluation. A few factors that secretaries consider particularly important are personal contact, problem-solving abilities, organizational skills, confidentiality, reliability, attitude, and commitment to the organization and its goals.

Try to Measure Your Secretary's Contribution to the Department in a Meaningful Way.   Be objective about the subjective. Use the *critical incident method* to capture the input and effectiveness of discretionary skills: Keep track or have your secretary keep track of actions that had particularly positive or negative consequences over the course of the appraisal period.

Here's an example that illustrates the importance of what we're talking about. A poorly written evaluation form will ask for a response concerning promptness and courtesy in answering the telephone. This broad question totally overlooks the fact that the secretary in question screens incoming calls from prospective clients. The secretary must use judgment in extracting information and deciding who can best help the caller. The secretary also must answer questions the caller may have, in effect serving in a sales and public relations capacity on behalf of the firm.

By asking such a basic question, the evaluation form does not take into account the volume of calls handled or the outcome of those calls: How many clients are added or lost by the company could in fact be partially attributed to the secretary. The secretary's performance in just this one area has an impact on the bottom line of the company. Evaluating that performance should somehow reflect the secretary's effectiveness in this respect.

Evaluation Should Focus on Results, not Methods. Criteria for evaluating secretaries often are irrelevant and even offensive to the professional secretary. A typical example is the question: "Is the secretary away from the work area longer than necessary?" Questions like these make the secretary feel like an assembly-line worker rather than a professional. How many pressure deadlines a secretary was able to meet versus how many were missed is far more indicative of performance than how many minutes a secretary was away from his or her desk. What should matter is what is produced, not how it is produced. Allowances should be made for variations in work style.

Undue Weight Should not Be Given to Punctuality and Absenteeism. One secretary complained that in her last performance review, all but 10 minutes of a 1-hour interview were spent discussing the fact that she was often 5 or 10 minutes late in the morning. No mention was made, however, of the fact that she often worked through lunch of her own accord or stayed 15 or 20 minutes late in the evening to tie up loose ends. As brought up in Chapter 1, this is an example of why secretaries don't feel like team members.

Most secretaries are unaware of federal laws that may dictate company policy concerning hours of work and overtime. If this is the case and federal restrictions are being appropriately applied, perhaps secretarial education in this area may be necessary. In the absence of such restrictions, it may be helpful for the secretary to keep track of merit points for good behavior that can counterbalance demerits received for being late or absent. In any event, these details should not take precedence over overall contribution.

Involve the Secretary in the Appraisal Process.   Suggest that your secretary keep his or her own evaluation documentation—a sort of daily journal already discussed. This makes the boss's job easier and helps ensure that secretaries have a realistic perception of their performance. You also can have your secretary fill out a self-evaluation form based on the appraisal form you use. You can then compare responses and clear up any misperceptions that may exist.

Performance Appraisal Should not just Evaluate Past Performance, but Provide Guidance for Improvement in the Future.   You know all about MBO—Management by Objectives. This management technique should not be reserved exclusively for management personnel. Use it with your secretary. Work together to set performance goals and plans for your secretary's growth and development. Think of your role in the process as coach, not judge.

The Results of a Performance Appraisal Should Be Shared with a Secretary by the Boss.   For a review to be meaningful, the secretary should be allowed the opportunity for mutual discussion of the appraisal. Don't leave the interview to personnel—bringing in a third party puts a wedge between secretary and manager that undermines the team spirit of the relationship. Schedule a specific time for the interview and ensure it will be uninterrupted. Accord your secretary the same courtesy you would a client or colleague.

Counteracting Other Organizational Problems

If your company tends to overlook secretaries, help your secretary gain positive visibility with upper management. Bring your secretary's accomplishments to the attention of key people within the company. Bringing talent to light can only reflect well on you. Make sure upper managers are aware of your secretary's professional development efforts. See that they know about degree work, the accumulation of continuing education credits (CEUs), or the attainment of the Certified Professional Secretary (CPS) rating.

If you come up against a stereotypical attitude about secretaries that seems unwavering, take the approach that your secretary is different. For example, if you seek a promotion for your secretary and meet with resistance because "secretaries are not promotable," insist that your secretary is an exception.

If your company does not get involved in career planning for the secretarial staff, do the counseling yourself. Using tools already mentioned, such as a job description and the performance appraisal, help your secretary develop a long-range career plan. You may worry you'll lose a good secretary down the road, but it doesn't mean it will happen overnight. Your efforts will go far in motivating your secretary to be of the utmost value to you in the meantime. Who knows? You may be able to promote your secretary within your own department and not lose him or her after all.

If general company practices tend to isolate secretaries, question whether such practices are written in stone. Just because secretaries are not usually invited to gatherings or included in meetings does not mean they are forbidden to attend. Take the initiative and bring your secretary along.

Your efforts to keep your secretary happy in a less-than-perfect business world cast you in the roles of mentor, coach, career counselor, and benefactor. These roles require little more from you than serving as catalyst and guide in your secretary's efforts toward career satisfaction. Each role adds a dimension to the secretary/manager relationship and develops the kind of loyalty that will benefit you as much, if not more, than your secretary.

CHAPTER SIX

THE WOMAN MANAGER

The evolving secretary/manager relationship is complicated, yet even more so for the woman manager. But, attention male readers—this chapter applies to you, too. Chances are you are directly or indirectly involved with a female secretary/manager relationship or will be. Whether you supervise women managers or share a secretary with one, you need to understand the dynamics of this special relationship.

It's a relatively simple matter to analyze the traditional male manager/secretary relationship because of its long history. It's more difficult to make generalizations about the female boss because women haven't been bosses long enough for patterns to develop. At this point, secretaries' perceptions about working for a woman tend to reflect individual experience rather than to broadly illuminate how the relationship is different.

It is possible, however, to point out potential problem areas from the woman manager's point of view. Women are not having an easy time moving into the management ranks of a male-dominated business world. In addition, secretaries are struggling to overcome a stereotype that has too long excluded them from their rightful place on the organizational team. The underlying issues of both campaigns collide when it comes to building and maintaining a successful secretary/manager team.

Problems between women managers and secretaries can become most acute when the manager finds herself in a woman-to-woman secretary/manager relationship. Woman-to-woman dynamics mix and mingle with all other factors, complicating relationships and often confusing issues. This chapter will focus on the common situation (97 percent of the time) where the secretary is also a woman.

Woman-to-Woman Dynamics

An eye-opening, realistic, though often unflattering view of how women relate to one another in the workplace is set forth in the revolutionary book, *Women vs. Women,* by Tara Roth Madden.

The premise of the book is that there is an uncivil war going on among women that keeps them from getting ahead in the business world. The culprit is not, as most women assume, the men in power. Madden's well-documented observations illustrate how women consciously and unconsciously sabotage one another's attempts to climb the corporate ladder. The book is instructive for a woman manager seeking to successfully relate to a woman secretary.

Learned Rivalry

Madden points out that women are socialized from birth not to support one another but to compete—elbows out, yet with a smile. In her words:

> Trained from infancy to view other women as rivals, they'd rather give up everything than take the chance of allowing other women to better them. At anything—prestige, friends, clothes, mates, or jobs. . . . That may be the call of nature. It is certainly the nature of the current struggle of women fighting women.[1]

This rivalry sets the stage for potential trouble between a woman manager and her secretary. A secretary may covet the manager's status, salary, office, and place among the elite, which is perhaps most significant from a secretary's perspective. The result may be an outwardly negative attitude toward a manager. The secretary may think, "She's not any better than me. Why shouldn't I have what she has?" This mindset ignores the obvious logic that these rewards must be earned. A secretary may feel "it's just not fair."

Such negativity can translate into active resistance where the manager seeks cooperation. More subtly, underlying envy, whether recognized or not, also can color a secretary's perception of a woman boss and heighten her sensitivity to what may be considered unsatisfactory behavior on a manager's part. Understanding the sources of this sensitivity is a way to start overcoming it.

Rivalry also can undermine relationships. According to Madden, the operative rule among women is, "Hold firm to your

---

[1] *Women vs. Women,* Tara Roth Madden (New York: AMACOM, a division of American Management Association, 1987), p. 68.

own small place in the universe and fight off any rivals who dare to invade your turf." A woman manager may catch herself reacting to a secretary as a threat to her position. The *Working Woman* survey discussed in Chapter 3 provides a statistic that may reflect the rivalry issue from both perspectives: more than 17 percent of responding women managers versus 5 percent of men answered yes when asked the question, "Do you ever get the feeling that your secretary thinks he or she could do your job?"

A secretary will not work well with a manager who takes pains to keep the secretary out while what she wants is to be drawn in as a part of the team. It's impossible for a manager to be an effective leader and mentor if she is unconsciously driven by the desire to keep the secretary down and out of the way. Look for your own tendency to feel threatened by your secretary and determine whether the threat is real or imagined. If your secretary is really out to get you, that's one thing. But if it's just learned rivalry keeping you at odds, call a truce and let it go.

The Secretary's Self

Madden's research confirms that self-image is a big issue in the war among women. As already discussed, self-image is an especially vulnerable area for many secretaries who feel the weight of the "just a secretary" stigma. Further, fueled by nagging doubts that a woman is measured by her career success (thanks to the women's movement), the daily presence of a woman who's made it beyond secretarial work can be a continual thorn in a secretary's side, even though she may be truly content with the work itself.

The problem, as Madden sees it, is that women just don't support one another's self-image. It may all go back to the rivalry issue. As one secretary, Sharon, puts it:

> Women have to be careful working with other women. Fran [Sharon's boss] has problems with people—women—who are not sure of themselves. Unfortunately, it seems if it's a male boss and the secretary is unsure of herself, then it's just the normal "male is better than female" type of thing. It sounds awful, but it's still true. Fran comes on too strong—her self-assurance can be intimidating. Her conflicts are always with women—never with men. I'm okay with her

because I have a lot of self-confidence, but I've seen her lose clients because the client contact was a woman.

A woman manager must consciously work at building the self-confidence of her secretary, not allow herself to unconsciously tear it down. Remember, women rate themselves by how they stack up against other women. If your behavior tells your secretary you're better because you're not a secretary, you effectively feed a secretary's (and a woman's) natural tendency to doubt her worth.

The Struggle for Priorities

Another potential trouble spot in the woman-to-woman secretary/manager relationship involves differences in values and priorities. Men generally agree that work comes first. Women's priorities are not so clear-cut and are apt to change with the ebb and flow of their personal life. Madden places working women in one of three categories:

☐ *Careerists:* Put business concerns above personal ones.

☐ *Balancers:* Desire harmony at home and at the office; office performance reflects the priorities of the moment.

☐ *Homing Pigeons:* Work because they must earn their way, but their primary energy is focused on leaving.

According to Madden, secretaries and managers alike fall into all three categories. Problems arise where both members of the team don't belong to the same category. Mixing two different value systems can create friction. There's also a tendency among women to consider their own choices right and people with different value systems wrong. Even more conflict and tension can result.

It should be clear between manager and secretary that all choices are right so long as one person's choice doesn't make someone else pay. All lines should be clearly drawn from the start, with mutual expectations known. As Madden aptly puts it: "Women's rules at work should be when at work, work comes first."

The Personal/Business Imbalance

Women are known for developing personal relationships with other women at the office. Rather than being perceived simply as a professional manager there to get the job done, the woman boss often finds herself cast in the role of mother, sister, or friend, says Madden. On the flip side, it's also probably true that secretaries are similarly cast in roles other than the key assistants they are meant to be. It's not hard to believe that the personal relationships common among women in the workplace "interfere with business and interfere with business decorum," as Madden suggests. One thing is certain, they can undermine the professionalism and effectiveness of the secretary/manager relationship.

Although she sometimes paints a grim picture of how women relate in the workplace, Madden does offer an interesting action plan for turning things around. One piece of her solution is particularly good advice for the woman manager attempting to build and maintain a successful secretary/manager relationship. Madden calls it "distancing." It's simple: separate business and social interaction with your secretary. Avoid "lunches, personal calls, coffee breaks, after-hours socializing, and office confidences about anything other than business." In short, be a manager, mentor, coach, and career counselor to your secretary, not a friend, sister, or mother. And look to your secretary as an able-bodied, key assistant, not a daughter, sister, or friend. Review Showing an Interest in Chapter 5 for tips on how to appropriately draw the business/personal line.

It's Been a Long, Hard Road

The woman manager has worked hard to earn a place on the management team, indeed, many feel even harder than her male counterparts. To some this has meant working longer hours, giving up more lunches, and working more weekends. Others have found it's not enough just to work harder; succeeding in a male-dominated management world often requires a woman to act like a man in order to fit in. For most women managers, personal sacrifices run high, but so do the rewards of success. A woman manager often rightly feels that she has arrived, perhaps against all odds.

A manager's own experience will consciously and unconsciously direct her behavior. The woman manager must be aware of how her actions may be received in order to avoid difficulty. Let's look at the woman manager from a secretary's point of view.

Who's Better than Whom?

It's often said that aggressiveness is considered a positive trait in men, but a negative one in women. Secretaries complain that some women managers seem to try harder to prove themselves and are pushy as a result. This may simply come from the secretary's preconceived notions about men and women, perhaps combined with woman-to-woman rivalry. But it also may be a manager's unconscious arrogance. Secretaries react negatively to women bosses who have a superior attitude—as though they're better because they have risen above secretarial work.

What causes a manager to be judged this way? Perhaps she's overly sympathetic, devaluing the work itself, or she may apologize too much for assigning what may be considered drudgery—copying, for example. Or perhaps she tends to go overboard in distancing herself from secretaries, as if being connected to them were detrimental to one's health. You must maintain a careful balance in the relationship. Being overly aloof is as bad as being too friendly.

Why Isn't She Like Me?

Often the same manager who is seen as pushy runs into trouble because she expects the same level of commitment in her secretary that she herself has shown in moving up the career ladder. Some women managers, especially those who were once secretaries themselves, take it for granted that secretaries are anxious to move out of the profession, always saying things like, "You're so smart—you can do better than this." One manager wrote to *Working Woman:*

> My secretary is a loyal, dedicated employee. I would love to groom her for a management position. Unfortunately, she is not interested in advancing to a decision-making role. She is proud to be an executive secretary—frustrating for a feminist boss![2]

---

[2] Kagan and Malveaux, *op. cit.,* p. 134.

A manager who openly expresses an attitude that feminism requires all women to share the same career goals may reinforce a secretary's nagging worry that it's not okay to be a secretary. One side benefit of secretarial work, that for some is a major impetus in making the profession a lifelong career, is that a secretary can be very close to the action without the weight of the responsibility that managers must bear. It doesn't suit some people, whether because of personality, lifestyle, or otherwise, to work at a job that goes home with you every night, if you go home at all.

You can't necessarily expect your secretary to share your drive. You can, however, impose your standards of excellence by insisting on the ultimate in professionalism.

It's true that some secretaries see women managers as more demanding than the traditional male boss. This can be a good sign. It sometimes means that, unhampered by stereotyping, a manager realizes a secretary is capable of more than typing. Women bosses also are sometimes called picky. The *Working Woman* survey revealed that secretaries to women managers report more conflict over work not being done fast enough or work mistakes than those with male bosses.

If you're considered demanding or picky, it may just mean your secretary has become accustomed to working for less-enlightened bosses who haven't expected that much from him or her in the past. As was said before, many secretaries also need enlightenment. It may be fair to say that women bosses in general are more enlightened than men—perhaps because so many rose from secretarial ranks themselves and know what a secretary can do. Many women executives do have secretarial roots. According to a recent survey of 142 women executives in New York City, 37 percent had their start as secretaries.[3] Nearly half of the women managers responding to the *Working Woman* survey already discussed were former secretaries.

There is a danger, though, especially among those former secretaries, of being *too* demanding and picky in what is perhaps a conscious or unconscious hazing ritual. Insisting on high performance standards is one thing, giving your secretary the same hard

---

[3] "Many Successful Women Started as Secretaries," *The Secretary*, June–July, 1987, p. 6.

time you may have experienced on your way up is quite another. As *Working Woman* advised in its survey report, "Just because you had to work for a so-and-so once doesn't mean *she* should have to."[4]

I Deserve Respect, Don't I?

Secretaries believe that some women managers demand respect—presumably based on the position they have fought so hard to gain. To a secretary, position alone does not merit respect; it must be earned, and the way to earn it is to exhibit respect for your secretary. Remember, respect is a very sensitive issue for secretaries. It's the first test a manager must pass in order to win the loyalty of a secretary and the last chance he or she will get if that test is failed. This is true whether a manager is male or female, of course.

Demanding respect can be the sure road to disaster, as Sally's story reflects. For 17 years, Sally was executive secretary to Jim, executive vice-president of a large department in a Fortune 500 company. Five years before Jim's retirement, a woman was hired to be groomed for his position. Meredith had great credentials. But by Sally's own description, she "had a lot of brains, but no smarts. She didn't know how to handle people on a one-to-one." Sally tells her story:

> At first, Meredith was pleasant and cordial, but then she started to bring out a chip on her shoulder—she didn't like taking orders or being told what to do. After a period of time she started showing evidence of an uncontrollable temper. Then she also began to be insubordinate to Jim—he would ask her to do assignments and she would refuse to do them. It was an awkward position for him to be in. I started complaining to Jim to do something about her. To me it was clear that Jim let her walk all over him because she was a woman in management, degreed, so therefore she was filling two quotas—hiring a woman, and hiring a degreed manager. Because she was a woman, he didn't make waves about her behavior. She was insubordinate—but he'd let it ride, give her another chance, and she'd walk all over him.
>
> Rather than asking me to do her work, she'd *insist* I do it. It was the way she asked—she demanded it be done. It was an automatic turnoff. And she demanded that I do her work *before* doing Jim's and, of course, my loyalty lies with him after 17 years. I wasn't going to let her push me around.

---

[4] Kagan and Malveaux, *op. cit.,* p. 109.

I had gone to Personnel a month or so before the big blow up to tell them that tension was growing and that it would eventually explode between us and it did. Her uncontrollable temper came out one afternoon. Something was bothering her—to this day I don't know what it was—something to do with a meeting she and Jim had earlier that day. She came out of her office, walked over to my desk, and pushed all the files on the floor. She didn't say anything. Just did it. I said, "What is your problem?" To this day I regret not making her pick up every piece.

We were screaming at each other. She was saying that things had to be done for her. She said, "I demand respect." I said, "You'll get it when you earn it." Then Jim came out to see what the commotion was all about, and she started yelling at him. "She did all the work and he got all the credit, she was getting fed up."

There was an investigation by the president's office. If I had started it, I probably would have been fired, but since Meredith started it she was just given a tap on the hand and told not to make waves.

Now things are different. She has Jim's job and I'm her assistant—no longer a secretary. Now she's a totally different person. Because she's in charge, she doesn't have to take orders from anyone except the president. Most of the time I have free reign to do my job without supervision. There are times when we have differences of opinion, but it's not as tense as it was before.

New roles, different relationship—overall, a not-so-unique story that teaches many lessons.

First, Meredith made a fatal error in not recognizing that she, Meredith, was effectively an interloper within a team with a 17-year history. Not only did she command that her work get done and that Sally put Jim's aside to do it, but she demanded Sally's respect as well. It just doesn't work that way. Maybe Sally was right—Meredith had no people sense. Common sense should dictate that the new kid on the block has to ease his or her way in to be accepted by the neighborhood.

In Meredith's defense, Sally really made no attempt to see things through Meredith's eyes. Meredith had a temper, yes, and there's no excuse for losing your cool. But there was obviously something happening between Jim and Meredith. Maybe she *was* up against a boss who saw her as a quota filler. It certainly would have been frustrating to work hard, feeling the necessity to prove her worth, and have Jim gloss over her contributions by presenting them as his own.

Speaking of Jim, his behavior might strike you as peculiar. What was he doing while Meredith and Sally were going at it? The fact that Jim did not intervene might be an example of another point made in *Women vs. Women*—that while women are at war, men often just observe from the sidelines. Catfighting is not seen by men as a managerial problem, but a female one. Madden would say Jim was probably thinking, "I wish you girls would get along and work things out."

Getting back to the women, Sally may have been more tolerant had she understood the situation from Meredith's perspective. To Sally, Meredith's behavior was astounding. "I don't understand what her problem was," she said. "She *had* Jim's job—she was hired specifically for it. It's not as if she were fighting ten people to get it." It doesn't appear that Meredith made any attempt to communicate with Sally on a meaningful level.

It would have been interesting to see what would have happened if Meredith had tried to help Sally see things from her point of view. Would Sally's loyalty to Jim have stood in the way? Would woman-to-woman dynamics have ruled—and Sally refused to support Meredith just because she was a woman? It's not easy to predict. The fact remains, Meredith did not choose to make the attempt.

And what about those unspoken issues? Isn't it interesting that Sally didn't seem to see anything wrong with considering Meredith a quota filler despite the fact that she recognized that Meredith was brilliant? Did unconscious rivalry move Sally to ignore Meredith's obvious ability? And how much of Sally's resentment had more to do with envy of her credentials and opportunity than her attitude?

When women work together, it can be complex. But let's get back to basics. The story provides an elementary lesson to all managers sharing a secretary whose first loyalty lies with another manager: Ask nicely for your work to be completed and you may be served. But a secretary may well consider it a favor, not your due.

I'm a Businesswoman First, Why Isn't She?

Women managers often find they must act like men in order to succeed. This means showing a concern for work above all, to the exclusion of home and family—at least outwardly. As one former secretary who became a manager and now is an expectant mother reports:

> I left my job when the company was bought out. Although I was offered a position with the new headquarters office, I chose not to move to another city. I had it in the back of my mind that it might be a good time to start a family, but of course didn't give that as a reason. Now I really wonder what Marty [her former boss] and the rest of the people in the department are thinking about me when they hear through the grapevine that I'm expecting. I was always so gung-ho career—if anyone mentioned babies, I'd worry aloud about what it would do to my career path. I realized it was an unwritten rule that I should say that, even if I didn't completely feel it, if I wanted to get ahead.
>
> I ran into trouble when I expected the same behavior from my secretary, who was pregnant during my last six months with the company. She was so openly preoccupied with preparing for the baby and it bothered me that she didn't give 100 percent to her work. But then I realized that rule just doesn't exist among secretaries—because no matter how you look at it, it's still a female-dominated profession. It didn't seem fair, yet I understood where it came from, having been there myself.

Here's an area where women managers and secretaries often clash. A female secretary may expect a manager, as another woman, to be sympathetic to personal demands. On the other hand, women managers forced to suppress family concerns in order to fit in a male-dominated arena may expect secretaries to do the same. Who's right? Are secretaries merely naive to the politics of career success? Or are women managers buying into male domination by trying to be something they're not? The answer to both questions may well be yes, but that doesn't mean either point of view is right or wrong. It's just a reflection of reality. Until society works out this problem, what's important is that manager and secretary come to terms with what they expect of each other in their own circumstances.

I Get the Feeling She'd Prefer to Work for a Man

With so much emphasis today on equality for the sexes, why does it sometimes seem that women secretaries prefer working for men? Secretaries may outwardly cheer for feminism, but as you can see, the women's movement has made life uneasy for them in several ways: Changing roles require a totally new outlook and pattern of behavior, women entering managerial ranks puts heightened pressure on how those roles must evolve, and a secretary's very choice of career is put in question. If some secretaries do prefer working with men, it's probably a natural resistance to change more than anything else.

It should be pointed out that in the *Working Woman* survey mentioned in Chapter 3, 49 percent of responding secretaries said it doesn't matter whether a boss is male or female. Further, a majority of both secretaries and bosses responded that women get the same amount of cooperation as men. One secretary was quoted as saying, "Any smart man or woman in authority can get help, cooperation, dedication, and loyalty from subordinates by treating them with respect. . .a professional secretary would not discriminate between men and women bosses."[5] This reflects the ideal, yet in reality it's clear that many secretaries do have a preference for a male boss.

As secretary/manager roles evolve, some secretaries find more comfort in clinging to the old than plunging into the new. It's scary for a secretary to be independent and assertive, especially when she gets little or no support from those around her. It's a lot easier to be dependent on and taken care of by a boss, especially if it's a traditional male boss who's also more comfortable to leave things as they've always been. Even if the old ways are unsatisfactory, it's just easier to go with the flow than to make waves.

To secretaries who are actively struggling to gain enlightened treatment, it may still seem safer to endure the turbulence of an evolving relationship with a male boss than to

[5] *Ibid.,* p. 108.

venture into uncharted waters. It's difficult to work with a woman manager because there's no past practice to fall back on, good or bad. A secretary may naturally try to work with the manager by relating to her as a woman. But as we've seen, there are many built-in pitfalls to that approach. While it may be accepted on an intellectual level that men and women should be equal in the workplace, it's not true in practice.

It's still the norm to see men in management positions, moving up the organizational ladder, getting bigger and better offices, gaining more power, and making more money. To many people, secretaries included, it's unfortunately rare to see or even expect women to do the same thing. A secretary may unconsciously look at a male boss and not think twice about what he has attained. But if the manager is a woman, she may begin to think, "I could have that if I weren't a secretary."

Secretaries may cheer for women who move up in their company. But when a secretary is assigned to such a woman manager, she must face head-on the implications of her career choices. Familiar doubts can begin to dance around in the secretary's head: "She's better than me because I'm just a secretary," or "I'm not successful because I'm just a secretary."

Isn't it interesting how men are not penalized for choosing not to shoot for the CEO position? When it comes to men, people realistically observe that there isn't room at the top for everyone. But society's current emphasis on equality for women somehow relays the message that unless a woman strives for the top, she's not serious about her career. Talk about a double standard. This is what secretaries are up against.

It's probably just a matter of comfort or, more accurately, the illusion of comfort if it seems secretaries prefer men. As pointed out, there's no reliable pattern—a secretary's perception of working with a woman manager is based on individual experience. A consultant who responded to the *Working Woman* survey was quoted as saying, "Most secretaries (female; I have no experience with male) are much more hesitant to work for a woman boss, sometimes because of past experiences. . . . I have also found, however, that once a good relationship develops, a secretary will prefer working for a woman." Let's hear why some secretaries do prefer a woman boss.

Making It Work

We've discussed the potential traps that can impede the success of the woman manager/secretary relationship. We've also mentioned several advantages the woman boss can bring to the relationship. Let's elaborate on these advantages and put it all together.

It's been pointed out that many women bosses had their start in the secretarial ranks. If you're one of those, draw on that experience. The former secretary is aware of how a secretary can contribute and thus may be inclined to assign more than the usual "secretarial" types of tasks—a definite plus. The exception may be women who have a difficult time delegating either because they view it as dumping on a secretary or because they fear losing a piece of their work. Remember, a secretary often craves the opportunity for more responsibility. Your guilt feelings probably are unfounded. As for feeling you must do it all yourself, remember what management means: getting things done through other people. You still get credit for work successfully performed under your supervision and you get the added benefit of motivating your secretary at the same time.

Having been in the trenches, so to speak, former secretaries may be more sensitive to the pet peeves of secretaries; for example, many secretaries observe that women bosses are less likely to require the performance of personal-service types of tasks. *Working Woman's* survey provided statistics to support this contention (see following page). Again there's nothing wrong with personal service so long as a secretary knows from the start that it's a part of the job. The fact remains, however, that many secretaries appreciate letting go of that part of the job for the sake of a contemporary view.

Secretaries report that working for a woman boss has its advantages even if that boss was never a secretary. For one thing, many secretaries find women bosses to be more considerate and less likely to procrastinate or assign work at the last minute. And despite the differences among women in how they set their work, family, and personal priorities, secretaries report that women better understand a secretary's outside demands.

Male Bosses Get
More Personal Service

When asked, "In your office, which of the following tasks are secretaries expected to perform?" secretaries' answers tend to differ according to whether they work for a man or a woman.*

	Secretaries with	
	Male Bosses	Female Bosses
Take dictation	74%	60%
Clean coffeepot	48	32
Sharpen pencils	46	41
Make personal arrangements for boss	40	29
Run personal errands for boss	39	37
Get boss's lunch	30	27
Balance boss's checkbook, pay his/her bills	14	6

*14% of secretaries surveyed have female bosses.

Reprinted with permission from *Working Woman* magazine. Copyright © 1986 by Working Woman, Inc.

Here's a story that gives a secretary's view of how women managers can be successful. Janet has worked for not one, but two women managers for three and a half years. She gives a glowing report:

> First of all, they are women, and smart as they are, they are a thousand times better than the men I have worked for. They're always fair and they treat me like a person. They have never ever missed an occasion, like Secretaries Day or my birthday. Once I was away for three days and they even gave me "welcome back" flowers on my return. They're so much more appreciative than any of the men I have worked for in the past.
>
> It's my bosses as individuals, though—not all women. There are some other women here who are equal to them in power, but I don't think I could ever work for them because of their attitude. I don't know these women, but from my observations, they seem bitchy—like they're power tripping. It's a kind of smugness. They're not friendly or nice, they never smile.
>
> Susan and Maura are definitely exceptions because they're both such good people as individuals and because they're so intelligent. They know how to deal with people and gain

loyalty. Some I attribute to their being women. The other part is just that they're so smart.

The women part is the sensitivity, nurturing, things in common, just life and the things we like to do—playing sports. I have something in common with both of them so there are things we can talk about and feel comfortable with each other. It's an office friendship. I don't see them outside the office except when they take me out for different occasions or when I work late, Maura drives me home because it's on her way and we talk—about work, about our lives.

It's really perfect—almost too perfect, because I have ambitions—I'd like to get into Administration, but the only way I could advance is to leave, and since they're so good, I don't have the motivation to leave. It's certainly not a bad thing, but you can get very comfortable.

It's obvious that these women managers have found just the right balance of mixing business and personal in the relationship. Perhaps because of this balance, there seem to be no undercurrents of rivalry among them. It would appear that communication is open, honest, and meaningful. They've also hit on a major key to success with secretaries—appreciation and recognition. Janet feels valuable and a part of the team, so much a part that she feels torn about leaving, although after three and a half years, some part of her feels it may be time to move on.

It's good to hear that at least *some* of the socialized qualities of women—consideration, nurturing, sensitivity—can have a positive effect on the secretary/manager relationship. Janet also pointed out what was said before, that the success of the relationship depends on the individuals involved.

So it all comes back to you. A woman manager must strive, like her male counterparts, to develop a successful relationship on a one-to-one basis with her secretary. Here's a checklist specifically for the woman manager.

A Checklist for the Woman Manager

1. Recognize how woman-to-woman dynamics may be influencing your relationship. (Read *Women vs. Women* and suggest that your secretary do the same.) Seek to understand your secretary's perception of you and try to help your secretary accurately understand your situation. Open and honest communication is *crucial*.

2. Build your secretary's self-confidence. Respect her expertise and allow her to take pride in her work. If she's content with a supportive role, so be it. If she seeks to follow in your footsteps, be her coach and mentor—you can only look the better for it.

3. Don't impose your values on your secretary. Instead, be reassuring that his or her value system is acceptable. Agree that when at work, work comes first. Set up standards and limitations that take into account the specifics of your personal realities. Come to a workable agreement and stick to it.

4. Work toward an appropriate personal and business balance with your secretary. Don't be overly friendly or overly aloof. Avoid being cast in non-work-related roles and keep from doing the same to your secretary.

5. Watch out for trigger behaviors to which your secretary may be particularly sensitive:

□ Don't come on like gangbusters; let the relationship build on mutual respect at its own pace.

□ Don't be overly apologetic about assigning mundane tasks. *Working Woman* advises: "It may work well to stifle your instinct to apologize at the outset and turn it into plentiful thanks once the chore is done."

□ Don't patronize a secretary who doesn't share your obsession for climbing the corporate ladder. *Working Woman* calls this "careerist snobbery." As they aptly put it, "[your secretary] can be loyal and willing to work as part of your team without wanting to make herself over in your image."[6]

With awareness and conscious effort, a woman manager can not only build a successful, mutually beneficial relationship with a secretary, but perhaps even help to turn around what has too long been a negative sisterhood among women.

[6] *Ibid.,* p. 109.

CHAPTER SEVEN

A FUTURE PERSPECTIVE

This book has been designed to help today's manager survive the secretarial crunch and take best advantage of the secretary/manager relationship. With the right approach, you can attract and hold the elusive high-caliber professional in today's labor-short market and utilize your secretary's talents to help you get ahead in your own career.

This book has prescribed behaviors and action plans, but more important, it has shown you a new way of thinking. What we've really been talking about is a change in outlook on the secretary, the secretary's function, and the secretary's role in an organization. Some say that changing attitudes is difficult at best and can occur only slowly over time. But you don't have the luxury of time. Change is already happening all around you.

You may resist adopting this new perspective. Despite whatever problems you have had with secretaries, it still may seem easier to take the path of least resistance than to purposefully change direction. Stop and think about what may keep you from following the good advice you've received. Is it ego? Is it your unconscious expectation that a manager deserves a secretary as a perk and nothing more? Is it fear? Are you afraid that allowing your secretary to fully participate will somehow detract from your own work contribution? Or is it merely backward wishful thinking—that everything was fine as it was and we should just leave things alone?

Up until now, the difficulties you've experienced with secretaries may have seemed only a minor, though continual disruption to your work. But they are difficulties that will not go away. Secretaries will no longer accept things the way they once were, and the secretarial shortage won't vanish overnight. You're only at one point in a continuum of change. What you've learned in this book will only bring you to where you need to be right now, today, to succeed in a quickly changing business environment. What will the future bring?

Let's see how others' predictions for the business world to come might direct how you must interact with the secretary of the future.

Downsizing—Making America Lean and Mean

There is a trend already in full swing to eliminate what has been dubbed the *corpocracy* of American business—the corporate version of bureaucracy that many believe is a major reason for the decline of American competitiveness in world markets. Organizations in all industries are pruning their staffs and emphasizing human resource development so that every employee in the organization's human resource pool is fully utilized. Secretaries must be included in this trend. A manager with outmoded attitudes may be a roadblock to progress—and may well find himself or herself left alongside the trail rather than among the pioneers in the company of the future.

The "Baby Bust"

The shrinking corporation and the growing emphasis on human resource development are two of three trends forecasted by John Naisbitt and Patricia Aburdeen in *Re-Inventing the Corporation*. The third trend is the coming seller's market created by the "baby bust" generation. It is significant here because it magnifies the number one problem with secretaries—the shortage of them.

Naisbitt and Aburdeen point out that during the 1970s companies had the luxury of being choosy about whom they hired because of the baby boom and the increase in the number of women entering the work force. During that decade, the number of people in the 18 to 24 age group—from which most corporations recruit their entry-level workers, including secretaries—increased 22 percent. In the 1980s that age group will decline by 15 percent, and by 1990 there will be 4.5 million fewer entry-level workers than in 1980, according to the U.S. Census Bureau.

Naisbitt and Aburdeen believe that economic growth will continue meanwhile, with new jobs far outnumbering people entering the work force. The result is a seller's market. Corporations will find they must compete for fewer top-notch, talented employees.

And what about the career choices of those entry-level workers? The coming generation has been described as the best educated, most independent, entrepreneurial, and self-reliant in American history. How many new workers do you think will choose a career that offers low status, little pay, and no opportunity for growth? Clearly, a new perspective is not a matter of choice.

The Information Age Meets the Electronics Age— The Future Nature of Work

Maybe some part of you still thinks the secretary will be eliminated by continuing advances in technology. After all, many managers already do their own typing on desktop computers, and before you know it, many predict, computers also will take dictation, transcribe and type letters, take telephone messages, schedule appointments, and do filing. Yet according to others, more evidence points to the demise of the middle manager than to the extinction of the secretary.

Naisbitt and Aburdeen point out that "[worldwide], middle management has shrunk more than 15 percent since 1979," and they expect this trend to continue. They further state:

> Middle managers. . .are losing out to smart technology in the race for productivity. Middle managers have benefited from the belief that people work better when they are closely supervised. But now those hierarchies which middle managers held in place are breaking into a wide array of largely self-managing structures. . . .
>
> Self-management is replacing staff managers who manage people; the computer is replacing line managers who manage systems. What really enables us to shrink middle management is the computer, which gives top executives immediate access to the information previously obtained from middle managers.[1]

You might expect this line of thinking to transfer over to the secretary/manager relationship. If computers give instant access to information, why won't a manager be able to gain needed information directly, without the help of a secretary? According to Paul Strassman, author of *Information Payoff—The Transformation of Work in the Electronic Age,* a manager's ability to independently read, process, store, and retrieve the information necessary to accomplish

---

[1] *Re-Inventing the Corporation,* by John Naisbitt and Patricia Aburdeen, Warner Books, Inc., pp. 12–13.

his or her work goals will be precluded by its sheer volume. Strassman had these words for secretaries attending Secretary Speakout® '87[2] on the topic of "Knowledge Management: Opportunity for the Secretary of the Future":

> In 1992 there will be 1.5 trillion pages of reading generated—24,600 pages for each information worker. If we don't deal with that, nobody will be able to understand what all of this information means. Nobody will be able to find the one page he wants.
>
> Executives do not have the basic skills or interests to deal with records.... Unfortunately, however, when they go to meetings, they have to go prepared, because increasingly the people who are on the other side of the table come with well-organized notebooks. Executives cannot walk into negotiations any more and just play it by ear. It is becoming very important to have briefings about who called whom, who said what, what document recorded what, and who approved of what.
>
> The business environment is becoming much more like library or legal environments which require enormous research and organizational skills.[3]

Strassman calls the secretary the "gatekeeper of electronic channels" and foresees the secretary in the role of "knowledge manager." In his words:

> As the office environment goes electronic, the key to [the secretary's] success will be the connections [they] make between phone calls, messages, scheduling, filing, typing, and copying, because what creates value is not those individual functions, which are electronically displaceable, but [the secretary's] ability to put them together for a particular use.
>
> Information management/retrieval is a discipline of great consequence, and it is not simple.[4]

---

[2] Secretary Speakout is a trademark of Professional Secretaries International. For further information on what comprises Speakout events, see the Appendix.

[3] *The Secretary,* June–July 1987, pp. 14–15.

[4] *Ibid.,* pp. 14–17.

What's the bottom line? Outside forces—downsizing, an information blitz, the electronics age—will make it even more difficult for a manager to keep a foothold in the corporation of tomorrow than that of today. That you'll need a top-notch person at your side will be even more true in the future than it is today. Your future career success may well depend even more on the support of a highly qualified secretary than you ever imagined. You can't hide your head in the sand on this one.

Something has to be done to attract the best and the brightest secretaries to your camp. And something has to be done to encourage students to enter the secretarial profession. The responsibility is yours—if you care about your own career.

Enhancing the Image of the Secretarial Profession

You're convinced, but where to begin? The profession is enhanced by everyone whose actions represent a contemporary perspective of the secretary as a valued, significant member of the organizational team. Here's a summary of how you can lead the way in your company by your action if you're in a position to act or by spreading the word if broad actions are beyond your control.

Secretary Speakout, previously mentioned, is a symposium to advance the secretarial profession that culminates in a consensus of required action or appropriate strategies to achieve identified goals. The consensus statement from Secretary Speakout '87 held in Atlanta, Georgia, in April 1987, and co-sponsored by Professional Secretaries International, the National Association of Educational Office Personnel, the National Association of Legal Secretaries, and the National Association of Rehabilitation Secretaries, assigns the following responsibility to the manager who seeks to enhance the secretarial profession:

> The profession now mandates: Employer responsibility for providing training, developmental opportunities, and financial assistance; communicating organizational goals; and

restructuring positions for competent secretaries to move up rather than out of the profession.

This is confirmation of what has been said all along: To win with secretaries, management must provide opportunities for career development and draw in the secretary as a part of the organizational team.

Professional Secretaries International and similar associations have many programs and activities already in place designed to enhance the profession. See the Appendix for details.

Attracting the Best and the Brightest

With the right approach, management can serve itself while simultaneously benefiting the entire profession. Specifically, managers and their organizations can attract the best and brightest by:

☐ Developing accurate job descriptions for specific secretarial positions.

☐ Assigning appropriate titles to positions rather than labeling all support staff *secretaries* or using broad categories that do not accurately reflect the function of individual secretaries.

☐ Basing secretarial salaries on position value and individual performance rather than tying salaries to the level of manager to whom the secretary reports.

☐ Restructuring secretarial career ladders to provide for career growth.

☐ Providing training for the secretary's professional development.

☐ Establishing appropriate recognition programs for secretarial contributions to organizational goals.

☐ Supporting secretarial involvement in professional associations that provide for growth and development.

☐ Opening communication channels to bridge the management/support staff gap and to provide a forum for problem solving among secretaries and managers.

These same actions are not only marketing tools for bringing in new secretaries, they also serve as strong methods for secretarial retention. A well-balanced, progressive action plan can net your company heightened morale, increased productivity, reduced turnover, and lower costs resulting from the negative effects of support staff dissatisfaction. This is winning all around.

Encouraging Students to Enter the Profession

Intensive marketing efforts are required to educate students about what secretarial careers have to offer—in general and within specific industries and organizations—and to convince students that secretarial careers are worth considering. It may well be worth your effort to get involved in such marketing efforts. Here's where you can turn for help.

The National Task Force on the Image of the Secretary was created in 1980 to bring together educators and the business community to find solutions to the growing secretarial shortage. The task force is a coalition of associations and organizations, including the Association of Independent Colleges and Schools, the National Business Education Association, the American Vocational Association, and Professional Secretaries International.

The activities of the task force focus on making educators, career counselors, and managers aware of the career opportunities available to secretaries and on emphasizing the importance of the secretary to business. The task force theme is "Secretary: A Career of Distinction. BE ONE!" Its mission is "to enhance the image of the secretary by attracting qualified individuals to the secretarial profession and by promoting the career opportunities that exist in the field." See the Appendix for further details.

Predictions

The Women's Movement Takes Another Turn

For any major social movement to be successful, a handful of fervent proponents must take an extreme position in order to bring the masses to some acceptable midpoint. So it has proven with the feminist focus on career equality for women. For years women have been reading and hearing about having it all—career, home, husband, children—you name it, it's yours. The tune has been changing recently, however.

Many women who have foregone marriage and children in order to establish a career are looking around and wondering whether they've missed the boat of life. Some of those who waited to start families until they were well-established professionally have found it not so easy to conceive when it's convenient for their careers. Books and articles in popular women's magazines that not so long ago focused on teaching readers how to be superwomen now take the opposite stance—dubbing the former have-it-all approach to womanhood the *superwoman myth*.

Meanwhile, many women who believed in that myth have been tearing out their hair wondering why they can't seem to juggle two, three, or four lives when it's obvious that everyone else is doing it so well. And while some women have been thinking there's something wrong with them because they don't fit the feminist ideal, secretaries have been feeling guilty and insufficient because they haven't made a proper career choice. At what price comes change?

It's okay now for women to relax somewhat. Even if salaries have yet to get to the point of equality, at least it's pretty well established that women have the choice of entering any number of what used to be considered strictly male occupations. But that doesn't mean they *must* choose a nontraditional field to be considered a success.

As the women's movement turns this next corner, the secretarial profession in its evolutionary state may well prove to be an ideal career choice for the woman who seeks the balanced life. Like any other job, secretarial work has its ups and downs. But for the woman who seeks to make a serious contribution without sacrificing her personal life, if she can accept the realities of the job, the benefits may well be worthwhile.

Secretarial work swings on the momentary needs of a manager—that's a fact. A secretary to some degree is subject to the whim of a manager—that's the negative aspect. Yet he or she also works close to the action, often right next to the center of power, without bearing the kind of responsibility that an executive must shoulder. Properly managed, secretarial work can be stimulating, meaningful, and exciting while allowing a secretary to maintain a life outside the office. As the image of the secretary improves, the profession may offer just what many women are looking for.

A Unisex Profession?

Women are not the only ones who have been changing—there is also a trend among many men to seek a more balanced life. While it's still true that society expects men to consider careers first and foremost, more than a few men are taking a decidedly more active role in the family than ever before. As the status, rewards, and advancement opportunities of secretarial work increase, the profession might attract more men than ever before.

It's often pointed out that, realistically speaking, there just isn't room at the top for everyone. If downsizing trends continue to flatten pyramidal hierarchies, this will be an even more compelling fact of life. Values are changing; as men and women seek more balance in their lives, perhaps the logical approach to work may shift from going for the top to finding meaningful, rewarding work.

Can secretarial work be a unisex profession? Yes, but only if management's perspective on secretarial roles follows a progressive road. If secretaries can be drawn in as team members and afforded the same opportunities to contribute as other staff members, men may be willing to enter a company's human resource pool through this port of entry.

A New Management Perspective

Running American business lean and mean, moving from an industrial to an information economy, focusing on human rather than financial capital—these are all trends that can mean a bright future for the secretarial profession. To the organization with foresight, secretaries can be an ace in the hole. Like finding money in your pocket you didn't know was there, secretaries can be a source of talent for companies that's been available, though overlooked, all along. Only the most progressive managers and companies will gain this competitive advantage. It's up to you. Will you survive and benefit from the secretarial crunch?

Appendix

Following are professional associations and other organizations which can provide information and services or serve as a source of potential secretarial candidates:

Professional Secretaries International® (PSI)

"The voice of the secretarial profession...the first and foremost nonprofit association of more than 40,000 secretaries throughout the world," PSI "promotes competence and recognition of the profession." PSI has 709 chapters throughout the United States with members in virtually all industries.

PSI is an excellent source of potential candidates and offers many programs and activities through its various departments designed to enhance the image of the secretary.

Institute for Certifying Secretaries (ICS). This department of PSI prepares and administers the Certified Professional Secretary® (CPS) examination and promotes the CPS program. ICS is also developing a CPS recertification program, and a task force on entry-level certification has been appointed to complete research for the design of an entry-level competency examination for business use.

Institute for Educating Secretaries (IES). This department of PSI oversees PSI's two student organizations: the Future Secretaries Association (FSA), for high school students, and Collegiate Secretaries International (CSI), a new organization for postsecondary students.

PSI Research and Educational Foundation. This is an independent, nonprofit trust that coordinates and authorizes research, distributes findings, and provides public instruction related to the secretarial profession. It works with those conducting studies of the secretarial profession and collects data about the role of the secretary in a technologically oriented business environment, concentrating on the evolving changes in business organizations.

The PSI Research and Educational Foundation originated and sponsors the *Secretary Speakout* format for the discussion of secretarial issues. Speakout is a symposium of professional colleagues gathered to advance the secretarial profession by speaking out on selected relevant issues, culminating in a consensus of required action or appropriate strategies to achieve identified goals for the profession.

In addition, special task forces have undertaken several projects. Secondary and postsecondary school curricula are being formulated, and corporate chapters, such as at GTE Midwestern Telephone Operations in Westfield, Indiana, are being established. Also, PSI and a representative cross-section of personnel managers are developing a prototype secretarial job description—a comprehensive, versatile instrument applicable to a variety of office environments and expressing common denominators of secretarial responsibility.

For information on PSI and its programs, contact:

Professional Secretaries International
301 East Armour Boulevard
Kansas City, MO 64111-1299
(816) 531-7010

National Task Force on the Image of the Secretary

Brochures, posters, buttons, stickers, a videotape, and an annotated bibliography on the "Image of the Secretary" are available for promotion of the profession. You can obtain these and further information by writing or calling:

National Task Force on the Image of the Secretary
c/o AICS
One DuPont Circle, N.W., Suite 350
Washington, D.C. 20036
(202) 659-2460

Other Associations That Have Secretaries as Members:

National Association of Legal Secretaries
3005 East Skelly Drive, Suite 120
Tulsa, OK 74105

National Association of Rehabilitation Secretaries
633 South Washington Street
Alexandria, VA 22314
(703) 836-0850

National Association of Educational Office Personnel
Kathleen Twomey, Executive Director
1902 Association Drive
Reston, VA 22091

Desk and Derrick Club
P.O. Box 747
Shreveport, LA 71162

National Association of Secretarial Services
Frank Fox, Executive Director
240 Driftwood Road, S.E.
St. Petersburg, FL 33705

American Association of Medical Assistants, Inc.
20 North Wacker Drive, Suite 1474
Chicago, IL 60606

National Association of Executive Secretaries
Bobbie Tinder, Executive Director
3837 Plaza Drive
Fairfax, VA 22030

Society of Architectural Administrators
c/o Ardis Williams
Haines Tatarian Ipsen and Assoc.
442 Post Street, Suite 500
San Francisco, CA 94102

Executive Women International
Mary Johnson, Executive Director
Spring One Plaza
965 East Van Winkle, Suite 1
Salt Lake City, UT 84117

The National Association for Female Executives
1041 Third Avenue
New York, NY 10021

Index